EXECUTORS AND PERSONAL REPRESENTATIVES: RIGHTS AND RESPONSIBILITIES

by
Margaret C. Jasper

Oceana's Legal Almanac Series:
Law for the Layperson

2003
Oceana Publications, Inc.
Dobbs Ferry, New York

341.7305
Jus

Information contained in this work has been obtained by Oceana Publications from sources believed to be reliable. However, neither the Pub-
lisher nor its authors guarantee the accuracy or completeness of any information published herein, and neither Oceana nor its authors shall be
responsible for any errors, omissions or damages arising from the use
of this information. This work is published with the understanding that
Oceana and its authors are supplying information, but are not attempting to render legal or other professional services. If such services are required, the assistance of an appropriate professional should be sought.

You may order this or any Oceana publication by visiting Oceana's website
at http://www.oceanalaw.com or contacting Customer Service at
1.914.693.8100 (domestic or international) or 1.800.831.0758 (U.S. only).

Library of Congress Control Number: 2003109149

ISBN: 0-379-11376-7

Oceana's Legal Almanac Series: Law for the Layperson
ISSN 1075-7376

©2003 by Oceana Publications, Inc.

To My Husband Chris

Your love and support
are my motivation and inspiration

-and-

In memory of my son, Jimmy

Table of Contents

CHAPTER 3:
OPENING THE ESTATE

CHAPTER 4:
PREPARING AN INVENTORY

CHAPTER 5:
PROSECUTING AND DEFENDING
ESTATE CLAIMS

CHAPTER 6:
TAX ISSUES

CHAPTER 7:
DISTRIBUTING THE ASSETS AND CLOSING THE ESTATE

CHAPTER 8:
GOVERNMENT BENEFITS

ABOUT THE AUTHOR

MARGARET C. JASPER is an attorney engaged in the general practice of law in South Salem, New York, concentrating in the areas of personal injury and entertainment law. Ms. Jasper holds a Juris Doctor degree from Pace University School of Law, White Plains, New York, is a member of the New York and Connecticut bars, and is certified to practice before the United States District Courts for the Southern and Eastern Districts of New York, the United States Court of Appeals for the Second Circuit, and the United States Supreme Court.

Ms. Jasper has been appointed to the panel of arbitrators of the American Arbitration Association and the law guardian panel for the Family Court of the State of New York, is a member of the Association of Trial Lawyers of America, and is a New York State licensed real estate broker and member of the Westchester County Board of Realtors, operating as Jasper Real Estate, in South Salem, New York. Margaret Jasper maintains a website at http://www.JasperLawOffice.com.

Ms. Jasper is the author and general editor of the following legal almanacs: AIDS Law; The Americans with Disabilities Act; Animal Rights Law; The Law of Attachment and Garnishment; Bankruptcy Law for the Individual Debtor; Individual Bankruptcy and Restructuring; Banks and their Customers; The Law of Buying and Selling; The Law of Capital Punishment; The Law of Child Custody; Commercial Law; Consumer Rights Law; The Law of Contracts; Copyright Law; Credit Cards and the Law; The Law of Debt Collection; Dictionary of Selected Legal Terms; The Law of Dispute Resolution; The Law of Drunk Driving; Education Law; Elder Law; Employee Rights in the Workplace; Employment Discrimination Under Title VII; Environmental Law; Estate Planning; Everyday Legal Forms; Harassment in the Workplace; Health Care and Your Rights. Home Mortgage Law Primer; Hospital Liability Law; Identity Theft and How To Protect Yourself; Insurance Law; International Adoption; The Law of Immigration; Juvenile Justice and Children's Law;

Labor Law; Landlord-Tenant Law; The Law of Libel and Slander; Marriage and Divorce; The Law of Medical Malpractice; Motor Vehicle Law; The Law of No-Fault Insurance; The Law of Obscenity and Pornography; Patent Law; The Law of Personal Injury; Probate Law; Privacy and the Internet: Your Expectations & Rights Under The Law; The Law of Product Liability; Real Estate Law for the Homeowner and Broker; Religion and the Law; The Right to Die; Law for the Small Business Owner; Social Security Law; Special Education Law; The Law of Speech and the First Amendment; Teenagers and Substance Abuse; Trademark Law; Victim's Rights Law; The Law of Violence Against Women; Welfare: Your Rights and the Law; and Workers' Compensation Law.

INTRODUCTION

After a person dies, someone has to step in and take care of the deceased's personal and financial affairs. For example, bills and taxes must be paid, and property of the deceased must be distributed according to the decedent's will, or according to state law if the decedent failed to execute a valid will.

This responsibility is borne by the person named in the will, or appointed by the court, as the decedent's personal representative. The term "personal representative" has been adopted by the Uniform Probate Code to refer to the individual responsible for administering a decedent's estate, whether or not the decedent died intestate. The personal representative may be named in the will or, in the case of intestacy, appointed by the court or elected by the heirs.

Following the Uniform Probate Code, many state statutes have also adopted the term "personal representative" to replace the traditional use of the masculine and feminine terms—executor or executrix—to refer to the administrator named in a will, as well as the masculine and feminine terms—administrator or administratrix—to refer to the administrator of an intestate's estate. In accordance with this trend, the reader is advised that this almanac will use the term "personal representative" when referring to the executor or administrator of a decedent's estate.

This almanac presents an overview of the probate process, and discusses the rights and responsibilities of the personal representative in winding up the decedent's affairs. These tasks are numerous and varied, and, at a minimum, generally include filing the necessary court documents to prove the decedent's will; identifying and filing an inventory of the decedent's property; having the decedent's property appraised; paying the decedent's debts and taxes; distributing the decedent's property according to the will or state law; and providing an accounting to the court. The aim is to provide the reader with a basic understanding of the probate system and the role one must fulfill if called upon to participate as a personal representative.

Because uniformity has not yet been achieved among the states, the reader is advised to check the laws of his or her own jurisdiction pertaining to specific questions on probate law and procedure.

The Appendix provides resource directories, applicable statutes, and other pertinent information and data. The Glossary contains definitions of many of the terms used throughout the almanac.

CHAPTER 1:
OVERVIEW OF THE PROBATE SYSTEM

IN GENERAL

The term probate literally means "to prove." The technical meaning refers to the process of proving the validity of a will before a court—i.e., determining whether the will fulfills the legal requirements set forth by the state. However, as commonly used, the term probate refers to the administration of a decedent's estate under judicial supervision, even if the decedent died intestate.

There is much public dissatisfaction with the current American probate system. It is perceived to be a lengthy procedure rampant with fraud and greed. As further discussed below, in response to the public's aversion to the probate process, many individuals have moved towards avoiding probate altogether, using any number of probate avoidance methods in planning their estate.

Another problem with the American probate system is the lack of uniformity among the states, although the Uniform Probate Code (UPC), as discussed below, has provided a framework from which the states can work towards uniformity.

THE UNIFORM PROBATE CODE

The Uniform Probate Code (UPC) was drafted by the National Conference of Commissioners on Uniform State Laws and approved in 1969 by the American Bar Association in response to a public outcry for probate reform. The UPC's purpose is to simplify and make uniform the law of wills and estates among the states, and to promote the speedy, efficient and cost-effective administration of estates.

The majority of the states have not yet enacted the UPC in its entirety, although many states have adopted portions of the law or have enacted their own legislation patterned after UPC provisions. To date, the UPC has been adopted, at least in part, by 18 states.

It would be impossible to reproduce the entire Uniform Probate Code in this legal almanac. However, for the reader's reference, the Table of Contents of the Uniform Probate Code is set forth at Appendix 1 as a useful guide in locating specific sections of law within the UPC. An overview of the UPC's major provisions is set forth below.

Overview of the Uniform Probate Code

The UPC contains eight articles with numerous sub-parts, as follows:

Article I—General Provisions

Article I of the UPC is broken down into four sub-parts, and contains general information concerning the UPC, including the purpose of the UPC and rules of construction; general definitions of the terms used throughout; jurisdictional matters; and notice requirements.

Article II—Intestate Succession and Wills

Article II is the second largest article of the UPC. It contains nine sub-parts. Article II contains the substantive law concerning the execution of wills and intestate distribution.

Article III—Probate of Wills and Administration

Article III is the largest article of the UPC. It contains twelve sub-parts detailing probate procedures and administration of decedent's estates. Article III presents the UPC's version of the procedures discussed in this legal almanac.

Article IV—Foreign Personal Representatives—Ancillary Administration

Article IV of the UPC contains four sub-parts concerned with administration of the decedent's estate outside of his or her state of legal residence, and the appointment of a foreign personal representative to administer the ancillary estate.

Article V—Protection of Persons Under Disability and Their Property

Article V of the UPC contains five sub-parts concerned with the protection of persons who are disabled, e.g. by incapacity or minority, and the protection of their property, and provides for the appointment of guardians.

Article VI—Non-Probate Transfers

Article VI of the UPC contains two sub-parts concerned with the transfer of non-probate property during the administration of the decedent's estate.

Article VII—Trust Administration

Article VII of the UPC contains three sub-parts concerned with the administration of trusts, the duties and liabilities of the trustee, and the jurisdiction of the court in overseeing trust administration.

Article VIII—Effective Date and Repealer

Article VIII of the UPC provides for the effective date of the UPC and matters relating to amendment and repeal.

THE WILL

A will is the legal declaration of a person's wishes for the disposition of his or her possessions after death. The will provides for the distribution of the decedent's property to certain individuals, in the manner and proportion the decedent designated.

As more fully discussed in Chapter 2, the will also designates a personal representative to administer the decedent's estate. The decedent's will must be submitted to the court where the decedent legally resided within a certain time period after death for validation. It must be established that the will was executed by the decedent in conformity with the laws of the particular state in which the decedent had his or her legal residence.

There are certain requirements that must be followed in order to make a valid will, which may vary from state to state. Generally, in order to make a valid will, the decedent must have been of the required legal age and mentally fit when the will was executed. Each state has a minimum age requirement for making a will. The majority of states, as well as the UPC, designate age 18 as the minimum age for making a will.

There are also technical requirements for the drafting of a valid will, according to the applicable state law. Generally, the will must be typewritten, signed before two or three witnesses, and dated. The will must also include the appointment of the personal representative.

If there have been minor changes to a will, a separate document—known as a codicil—may have been drafted to make additions or deletions. In order to be valid, any codicils must have been executed in the same manner as the will.

In general, wills do not have to be notarized, but in some states, the witnesses can sign and have notarized a "self-proving affidavit," which eliminates the need for a witness to testify at the probate proceedings.

If the will is not self-proving, the witnesses who signed the will must attest to its validity and the decedent's signature. Affidavits must be signed by the witnesses and notarized. Once the sworn affidavits are returned, they should be filed with the court along with the will and any necessary forms for opening the estate.

Some courts require a hearing at which time the witnesses may be required to testify. If the will is not self-proving and the witnesses cannot be located, the testimony of other witnesses as to the authenticity of the signatures of the witnesses and decedent may be required.

DISINHERITANCE

With few exceptions, an individual is not required to leave any property to any person unless they wish to do so. Thus, if a person is not named in the decedent's will, they will have no claim to the decedent's property after he or she dies. For example, an individual is permitted to disinherit a child. However, the decedent's intention to do so must be clearly stated in the will to avoid a claim against the estate by that child.

In general, to disinherit a child, the will must either expressly state the decedent's intention to do so by including such a clause in the will, or by leaving the disinherited child a very small gift, such as one dollar, which, for all practical purposes, would constitute a disinheritance.

Disinheriting a spouse is more complicated. In the majority of states, one simply cannot disinherit a spouse unless the spouse waives his or her right to a portion of the estate. In the absence of such a waiver, the spouse is generally entitled to at least one-third of the decedent's estate.

Most states permit the surviving spouse to choose between the will provisions or receiving a certain portion of the estate according to the state's law. This is known as the spouse's right of election. The purpose of this law is to prevent a disinheritance of the spouse which might cause the disinherited spouse to become destitute. The portion of the estate available to a surviving spouse varies greatly from state to state, thus the reader is advised to check the law of his or her jurisdiction.

CONTESTING A WILL

In certain instances, a will may be contested. A will may be contested on either procedural or substantive grounds. Procedurally, if a will does not meet all of the legal requirements of the applicable state's statutes, it must be declared void. The most common substantive ground for a successful will contest is proof of the testator's lack of mental capacity at the time he or she executed the will.

In addition, if it can be shown that a will, or any of its parts, was executed under undue influence—i.e., by coercion or force—the will, or that part of it executed under undue influence, is void.

A person who wants to contest a will must file his or her objections to the will with the court within a certain time period after the personal representative has notified interested parties of probate. A formal hearing must be held by the court to determine the issues raised by the will contestant. The personal representative is responsible for defending the will's validity.

A successful will contestant generally receives that share of the estate he or she would have received under state intestacy laws. If the will contest concerns the validity of two or more existing wills, the successful will contestant will receive his or her share according to the will which is proven valid. In addition, a successful will contestant's legal fees are generally paid from the estate's assets. Thus, prolonged will contest litigation can seriously deplete the assets of the estate.

INTESTACY

If the decedent died without a will—i.e., intestate—his or her property will generally be distributed to the decedent's family members according to state law. This is a fairly common occurrence. Some people never consider making a will because they believe they have many years of life ahead of them or because they believe they have not accumulated enough assets to justify making a will. Others just never get around to making a will.

In some situations, the deceased may have executed a will, but later rendered it wholly or partially invalid by altering it. Any alterations made to a will after it is executed are prohibited without the attendant formalities. Further, if a will is successfully contested, the decedent will be deemed to have died intestate.

Intestacy procedures are determined according to the state in which the decedent maintained his or her legal residence. To begin the proceeding, the appropriate forms must be filed with the court in place of the will.

The court will then hold a hearing to appoint a personal representative to administer the decedent's estate. Some states permit the family members to elect the personal representative.

When it is determined that a person has died intestate, his or her estate must be distributed according to the state's statutes concerning intestate succession—the law of descent and distribution. Depending on the state, administration of the decedent's estate may require court supervision. ·

Although state statutes are not uniform concerning the manner of distribution, most state intestacy laws provide that the estate passes in varying percentages to the decedent's spouse and children. If the decedent was not married and had no children, the estate usually passes to the decedent's siblings and/or parents. Nevertheless, if the heirs can agree to a different division of the decedent's assets, the state distribution requirements may be waived.

A table setting forth the state rules of inheritance is set forth at Appendix 2.

When there are minor children involved, the court must appoint a guardian to care for the children and manage their inheritance until they reach the age of majority. The child's share of the estate is held in trust by the court-appointed guardian until that time. If there is a surviving parent, he or she is usually appointed as the guardian of the children's person and property.

ANCILLARY ADMINISTRATION

If a decedent owned property outside of his or her state of legal residence, a separate probate proceeding must be initiated. This is known as ancillary administration. Depending on the law of the state where the property is located, a personal representative may have to be named in that state to administer the assets located there.

PROBATE AVOIDANCE

Because the probate process can be time-consuming and expensive, there is growing support for probate reform. In the United States, there are legal mechanisms for property to bypass a will, also known as probate avoidance methods. Such methods may include naming beneficiaries to receive life insurance proceeds, and pension and retirement plan distributions; joint ownership of property; setting up living trusts; and informal probate avoidance procedures.

Informal Probate Avoidance

Families often resort to what is known as informal probate avoidance, whereby the family bypasses the court and independently divides the deceased relative's property as his or her will—if there is one—directs. If there is no will, the family may divide the property according to the state's intestacy statutes or by mutual agreement.

Informal probate avoidance often occurs when the decedent's estate is very small, generally consisting entirely of personal property that is accessible to the family members. However, if the decedent has left any property that requires legal authority to transfer title, such as a house, formal probate procedures must be followed to obtain the legal authority to transfer title.

Probate Exemptions

Some states provide various exemptions from the probate process by either allowing a certain amount of the deceased's property to be completely exempt from probate or subject to a much more simplified probate process than normal.

A table of state law exceptions to conventional probate is set forth at Appendix 3.

CHAPTER 2:
THE PERSONAL REPRESENTATIVE

IN GENERAL

The personal representative is the individual responsible for administering a decedent's estate, whether or not the decedent died intestate. The personal representative may be named in the will (also known as the "executor" of the estate) or, in the case of intestacy, appointed by the court or elected by the heir (also referred to as the "administrator" of the estate).

The personal representative may be a family member or friend of the decedent. If the decedent was married, the surviving spouse is usually appointed as the personal representative. In some cases, the attorney who drafted the will is named as the personal representative. Often, a bank or trust corporation will act as the personal representative of an estate, particularly a large estate with a number of complex assets.

Some states allow for the appointment of more than one personal representative, such as two family members. In addition, the decedent may have desired a family member to act generally as personal representative, but appoint a bank to handle the business aspects of the estate. Thus, the family member and the bank would be named in the will as co-personal representatives. In such a case, unless the will provides otherwise, both co-personal representatives must be in agreement and sign all documents in connection with the administration and distribution of the estate.

The individual named as personal representative in the will can decline to accept the responsibility. In most cases, there will be an alternate named in case the first choice declines to serve. However, if there is no named alternate, or the alternate also declines to serve in this capacity, the court will appoint a personal representative for the estate.

If the decedent did not leave a will—i.e., died intestate—the administration of the estate will take place according to the law of the state in which the decedent resided. In the case of intestacy, the court appoints an individual to act as the personal representative responsible for administering the estate. Sometimes the family members are permitted to elect a personal representative.

POSTING A BOND

A personal representative may be required to file a bond, equal in value to the decedent's estate, in order to protect the beneficiaries of the estate. For example, a bond may be required if the court so orders; if the will states that a bond is required; or if an interested person demands that a bond be posted and the court agrees. However, in most cases, if a family member is named as the decedent's personal representative, the will will dispense with the filing of a bond.

A sample fiduciary bond is set forth at Appendix 4.

QUALIFICATIONS AND RESTRICTIONS

A personal representative is not required to have any special legal or financial abilities because special tasks, such as accounting or investment management, can be delegated to qualified professionals who are paid from the proceeds of the estate. The most important qualifications a personal representative should possess are honesty and good organizational skills.

Although a personal representative may live in another state, some states require that he or she is a relative or primary beneficiary under the will. In addition, the nonresident personal representative may be required to post a bond to protect the beneficiaries. Further, minors, convicted felons and non-citizens are generally disqualified to act as a personal representative.

COMPENSATION

The personal representative, and the professionals hired by the personal representative to assist in administering the estate, are entitled to compensation for their services.

The Personal Representative

Most family members and close friends who agree to act as personal representatives for the estate do not collect a fee for their services. If they do collect a fee, it is usually a nominal amount.

If an attorney is named in the decedent's will to act as personal representative, or is retained by the family or appointed by the court to administer the estate, there will likely be fees incurred. Fees would also be payable by the estate if a bank or other corporation is named to serve as personal representative.

This is often the case when the estate is large and complex, and there are no family members or friends available or capable of handling administration. Unfortunately, this usually results in higher fees because corporations often hire lawyers to assist in the technical aspects of administration.

The personal representative's compensation is dependent upon a number of factors, including:

1. The total value of the estate;

2. The complexity of the estate;

3. The time spent by the personal representative in administering the estate;

4. The skill displayed by the personal representative in administering the estate;

5. The degree of care exercised by the personal representative in administering the estate;

6. The results of the administration, including any investments made by the personal representative.

Generally upon the closing of the estate, the beneficiaries are asked to approve the level of executor's compensation. If the beneficiaries do not agree, then the personal representative's compensation is fixed by the court.

The Estate Lawyer

An estate lawyer may be hired by the personal representative to assist in administering the estate, particularly when there are complex issues which need to be resolved. Some personal representatives hire a lawyer to oversee the entire probate process. The result is that the lawyer may charge a considerable fee—usually computed as a percentage of the estate—for performing duties which can easily be performed by the personal representative. As discussed below, it is more cost effective to the estate for the personal representative to undertake most of the probate work, and to retain a lawyer on an hourly basis for specific purposes as the need arises.

Qualified Experts

Administering the estate may necessitate the hiring of qualified experts, such as an accountant for the preparation of income tax returns.

The fees of such experts must be paid in addition to the personal representative's compensation.

Fee Limitations and Arrangements

In order to protect the estate from being depleted by excessive fees, laws exist which place a cap on the fees that can be charged for services performed. Nevertheless, the state's legally permissible fees, usually based on a percentage of the estate, can still be quite a drain on the assets of the estate.

In many cases, the fees charged do not adequately reflect the services which were performed. If a lawyer is hired to assist in probate, it is important that a written fee agreement be obtained prior to his or her rendering any services.

One must understand the manner in which fees for services rendered will be calculated so that a professional may be hired whose rates will be most cost effective. In general, fees are charged either on an hourly rate, or as a percentage of the estate.

An hourly rate may be the most advantageous fee structure because it reflects payment for actual work performed. Conversely, if the fee is based on a percentage of the estate, it will quite likely be disproportionate to the amount of work performed on behalf of the estate. It is customary in many states for probate fees to be computed on a percentage basis regardless of services performed, although many states are attempting to enforce a "reasonable fee" standard, particularly as it pertains to estate lawyers.

Fee Reduction

An interested person may file a petition with the court for a reduction in the fees charged by a personal representative or estate lawyer. However, it is often difficult to prove that the fee is unreasonable without documentation of the time and effort expended. If administration required mostly clerical work and the filing of forms, the petitioner may be able to show that, on an hourly basis, the requested fee is clearly disproportionate to the work performed.

The personal representative or estate lawyer must then demonstrate to the court how his or her fee is reasonable and customary. The court will review all of the evidence and testimony and render a decision. In the meantime, the closing of the estate and distribution of assets will be suspended while a fee reduction petition is pending.

RESPONSIBILITIES OF THE PERSONAL REPRESENTATIVE

In general, a personal representative is expected to settle and distribute the decedent's estate as quickly and efficiently as is consistent with the best interests of the estate. As further discussed in this almanac, depending on the complexity of the estate, administration of the decedent's estate may require the personal representative to undertake some or all of the following responsibilities:

1. Carrying out the written instructions of the decedent relating to his or her body, funeral, and burial arrangements.

2. Arranging for the immediate needs of survivors.

3. Locating the will and other important papers and information.

4. Making application to probate the will or to terminate joint tenancy or for appointment as personal representative.

5. Selecting an attorney to handle the estate, if necessary.

6. Giving legal written notice of his or her appointment to the heirs, if there is no will, or devisees, if there is a will.

7. Taking possession of estate property.

8. Notifying decedent's life insurance companies.

9. Paying expenses for last illness, funeral and burial expenses, and other debts.

10. Having real and personal property appraised.

11. Preparing and filing an inventory of all of decedent's property with the inheritance tax section and clerk of court.

12. Publishing a notice to creditors for debts of which the personal representative may be unaware.

13. Preparing and filing federal estate tax returns if the estate is subject to estate tax.

14. Preparing and filing state and federal income tax returns for the decedent's last year of life and, if necessary, for the estate.

15. Arranging for the family's immediate living expenses.

16. Determining which estate assets will be needed to pay state inheritance or federal estate taxes, if applicable, as well as administration expenses and other costs of settling the estate.

17. Satisfying charitable pledges in the decedent's will.

18. Ascertaining the values at date of death for all of the decedent's bank accounts, closing those accounts, and opening an estate account.

19. Depositing or investing liquid assets of the estate in federally insured interest-bearing accounts, readily marketable secured loan arrangements or other prudent investments, if funds are not needed to meet debts and expenses currently payable.

20. Distributing assets as required by law of intestate succession or by decedent's will.

LIABILITY ISSUES

The personal representative acts in a fiduciary capacity. Although the personal representative may not have to report to the court, he or she is fully accountable to the heirs. The personal representative has a duty to do what is reasonably necessary for the good of the estate and those who have an interest in the estate.

If the personal representative finds that he or she has a dispute or conflict of interest with any beneficiary of the estate, it is important to have all of the beneficiaries and/or the court approve any decisions or actions which could possibly be questioned and/or lead to personal liability.

Protection of Estate Assets

The personal representative is responsible for protecting and preserving the assets of the estate. Thus, he or she must be prudent in making investments, maintaining records, and ensuring that estate property is adequately insured, etc. If there is personal property, such as a car, the personal representative must make sure that the property is maintained and kept in a secure location. In addition, estate funds should be held in interest-bearing accounts.

Hiring Qualified Professionals

If the personal representative is not sufficiently qualified to handle specific matters affecting the estate, it is imperative to hire a qualified professional, such as a lawyer, accountant, or appraiser, to perform the particular task. Nevertheless, the personal representative is responsible for monitoring the professional's performance.

If the personal representative has experience handling certain matters, it is still prudent to periodically consult with a qualified professional in the particular area of expertise.

Making Investments

If the personal representative makes any investments on behalf of the estate, he or she must make sure that there is a balanced portfolio of investments, e.g., some should be income-generating while others may be capital investments, such as stock. Of course, as discussed above, the personal representative should hire a qualified financial advisor before making any investments.

Negligence

A negligence claim can be brought against the personal representative if he or she breaches their duty to protect and preserve estate assets. For example, if the personal representative makes unauthorized investments, and those investments lose money for the estate, the personal representative may be held liable for those losses.

In addition, the personal representative is advised not to make any speculative investments. In the event of a loss, the executor may be found liable to the estate for the entire amount of the loss including interest.

The personal representative may also be held liable for any losses the estate may incur if he or she fails to collect on debts owed to the estate; sells estate property without authorization; overpays a claimant or sells property at an inappropriate low figure; or distributes estate assets to the wrong beneficiary.

Liability for Unpaid Taxes

State laws may also hold the personal representative personally liable for unpaid taxes of an estate. Liability may arise, for example, if the personal representative pays claims out of estate assets before satisfying state tax debts. Consider the following Mississippi statute:

Mississippi Code: Section 27-9-37.
Personal liability of the executor.

Every executor, administrator, or assignee, or other person, who pays any debts, except as hereinbefore provided for, due by the person or estate from whom or for which he acts, before he satisfies and pays the tax due the State of Mississippi under this law, from such person or estate, shall become answerable in his own person and estate for the tax so due the state, or so much thereof as may remain due and unpaid, to the full extent of the full value of any property belonging to such person or estate which may come into his hands, custody, or control, and the executor shall in all instances be liable on his bond for the payment of the estate tax, whether the estate has been closed by the chancery court administering same or not.

Thus, a personal representative who distributes the estate prior to completion of the estate tax audit could become personally liable.

Releases

When distributing assets, it is important to have any beneficiary who receives a distribution of estate assets to sign a release. A release is a legal document which is signed by the beneficiary, setting forth the specific distribution of assets the beneficiary received, and stating that he or she has no further claims against the estate. This written acknowledgement provides the personal representative with some measure of protection should the beneficiary later assert another claim against the estate.

Compensation

There used to be a rule, which prohibited an executor from "pre-taking" compensation before it had been approved by the beneficiaries or fixed, by the court. This rule has been modified by recent court decisions. As a result, depending on state law, the personal representative may be entitled to "pretake" compensation before it has been approved by the beneficiaries or by the court.

Nevertheless, it is still generally prudent to obtain beneficiary or court approval before taking any compensation. In the event that compensation is pre-taken, if it is ultimately determined by a court to have been excessive, the executor will be required to pay the excessive amount together with interest.

Intermingling of Funds

The personal representative is absolutely prohibited from intermingling estate assets from his or her own personal assets. The estate account must be in the name of the estate, not the name of the personal representative. Further, estate funds must never be deposited in the personal representative's personal account. In addition, investments, such as stock certificates, must be held in the name of the estate.

Liability of Co-Personal Representative

If more than one person is named by the will to serve as a co-personal representative, he or she will be jointly responsible for all actions which negatively affect the estate, and jointly liable for any acts of the other co-personal representative that diminishes the assets of the estate.

Therefore, it is crucial for any person serving in the capacity of co-personal representative to obtain copies of all correspondence, bank statements, investment statements, etc. In addition, the co-representative should require that he or she be consulted in connection with any important decisions concerning administration of the estate assets. The co-representatives may agree that any major decisions can only be made in a signed writing.

CHAPTER 3:
OPENING THE ESTATE

IN GENERAL

It is the responsibility of the personal representative to make a formal application to the court for appointment, even when he or she has been named in the decedent's will. The form is commonly referred to as a probate petition. The petition is generally submitted to the court, along with the will and any other necessary documents, in order to "open the estate."

A sample petition for letters of administration is set forth at Appendix 5.

OBTAINING A DEATH CERTIFICATE

The personal representative will need to obtain a number of certified copies of the decedent's death certificate in order to carry out many of the tasks associated with administering the estate, e.g. to collect death benefits, insurance proceeds, etc. In most cases, the funeral director will obtain copies of the death certificate as part of their services.

If the funeral director does not obtain copies of the death certificate, of if additional copies are needed, they can generally be obtained in person, by mail, or online from the state office which handles vital records. When requesting the death certificate, the personal representative will generally have to provide some or all of the following information:

1. The decedent's full name.

2. The decedent's date of death.

3. The name of the city and county of death.

4. The decedent's social security number.

5. The decedent's place of birth.

6. The personal representatives authority to obtain the death certificate.

7. The personal representative's name, address and phone number.

In addition, the request should set forth the number of copies requested and payment to cover the fee for the copies.

Information on where to apply for a death, birth, marriage or divorce certificate in each of the 50 states is available online from the National Center for Health Statistics at the following website:

http://www.cdc.gov/nchswww/howto/w2w/w2welcom.htm.

SELECTING A PROBATE PROCEDURE

Under present law, probating a will is a largely administrative procedure. Depending on the size of the estate to be administered and the applicable state law, the personal representative generally selects a probate procedure. The three most common procedures are supervised, unsupervised and small estate administration. These three procedures are discussed in more detail below.

Supervised Administration

Supervised administration is the usual manner in which an estate is administered. The reader is advised to check the law of his or her jurisdiction concerning the availability of unsupervised administration. However, even in those states which permit both supervised and unsupervised estate administration, the court may require supervised administration if it determines that the personal representative is not qualified to act unsupervised.

Supervised administration merely dictates that, at certain stages of administration, the personal representative file the required forms with the court for approval. For example, the personal representative may be required to obtain court approval before distributing assets or paying claims. The personal representative may also be required, on occasion, to make court appearances.

Unsupervised Administration

Unsupervised administration is available in states which have adopted the Uniform Probate Code, and other states which have made specific provisions for it under certain circumstances. Unsupervised administration generally requires the consent of all interested parties, and an interested person may request the court to supervise either all or part of the administration of the estate.

Unsupervised administration is less formal and has few reporting requirements. In fact, once letters of administration have been issued to the personal representative by the court, the estate can be settled without further court intervention.

Small Estate Administration

Small estate administration refers to a simplified procedure for probating a small qualifying estate. In general, an estate qualifies for small estate administration in most states if (i) there is no solely owned real property; and (ii) the value of the estate does not exceed the state mandated maximum.

The monetary ceiling is based on the value of probate assets solely owned by the decedent. Jointly owned assets, insurance proceeds and other death benefits are generally excluded when valuing the estate to determine if it qualifies for small estate administration. Depending on the state, a number of additional exclusions may apply. Thus, an estate which at first appears too large for small estate administration may qualify once all of the exclusions are deducted from the value of the gross estate. The reader is advised to check the law of his or her own jurisdiction to determine the applicable exclusions.

If an estate qualifies for small estate administration, probate generally involves following several basic steps. The person handling administration of the estate is referred to as a claimant instead of a personal representative. In some states, the claimant must be a family member, such as the surviving spouse.

In general, there are two types of small estate administration: (i) summary administration; and (ii) administration unnecessary.

Summary Administration

Summary administration is a shortened probate process which generally requires the claimant to provide notice of administration to all interested persons. In addition, an inventory of the estate assets is usually required to be filed with the court.

Administration Unnecessary

Administration unnecessary does not, as the name implies, require any probate administration.

Small estate administration is generally accomplished by means of a (i) court order, or (ii) by affidavit.

Administration by Court Order

In states which require administration by court order, an inventory and appraisal of the estate's assets, and any other necessary documentation, must be filed with the court along with the petition for small estate administration.

If the petition is granted, the court will issue an order authorizing transfer of title, or the release of estate assets, to the claimant. The claimant presents the order to persons who are holding estate assets to obtain their release, or to whoever is responsible for transferring title to estate assets.

Administration by Affidavit

Most states simply require a claimant to complete an affidavit and file it with the court. The affidavit must be signed by the claimant and notarized. As with the court order, an original notarized affidavit is presented to persons who are holding estate assets to obtain their release, or to whoever is responsible for transferring title to estate assets.

NOTIFICATION REQUIREMENTS

The personal representative is responsible for notifying all interested persons about the individual's death. Such notification is generally required to be personally served or served by mail. Interested persons include but are not limited to beneficiaries, heirs and creditors.

According to the applicable statute, notice must be given within a certain time period, and must generally advise interested parties that the personal representative has applied to the court for formal appointment, and has opened the estate for probate. The notice should also include the name and address of the personal representative, and provide information on how interested parties can obtain a copy of the decedent's will.

The reader is advised to check the law of his or her jurisdiction concerning the manner and timing in which notice must be made.

A sample Notice to Creditors is set forth at Appendix 6.

Proper notice may also require publication in an approved newspaper circulating in the area where the decedent legally resided. Such notice serves to inform both creditors and interested persons of the opening of the estate.

A sample affidavit of publication is set forth at Appendix 7.

LETTERS OF ADMINISTRATION

Once the personal representative's petition for appointment has been approved, he or she is issued "letters of administration"—also referred to as letters testamentary—which serve as official proof that the personal representative is authorized to administer the decedent's estate.

A sample order approving the petition and issuing letters of administration is set forth at Appendix 8.

CHAPTER 4:
PREPARING AN INVENTORY

IN GENERAL

The personal representative is responsible for locating and preparing an inventory of all of the decedent's assets, and assessing the value of the estate. The personal representative must also attempt to take possession of all the decedent's property to be administered in the estate.

A preliminary estimate of the value of the decedent's estate may be required when the estate is opened. A preliminary estimate assists the personal representative in budgeting for the expenses of operating the estate during the administration process.

Further, depending on the preliminary valuation, the estate may qualify for small estate administration, a very simple process preferable to both supervised and unsupervised administration. Small estate administration is further discussed in Chapter 3.

LOCATING ASSETS AND DEBTS OF THE ESTATE

Within a certain time period following the opening of the estate, the personal representative must complete a more formal inventory and appraisal of the estate. A search for all of the decedent's assets, as well as debts, must be undertaken in order to properly inventory the estate.

If the personal representative is unfamiliar with the decedent's affairs, information concerning assets and debts may be ascertained by contacting the decedent's relatives, friends, employment and business associates, and banking institutions. All of the decedent's files should be searched for receipts, bills, loan papers, warranties or other evidence of assets and debts.

Along with his or her will, the decedent may have left an estate planning guide containing detailed instructions and information to assist the personal representative in carrying out his or her wishes.

A sample estate planning guide is set forth at Appendix 9.

To assist in the search, the following information should be ascertained:

1. The location of the original and any copies of the decedent's will.

2. The names and addresses of the person(s) the decedent designated as guardians of his or her minor children, if applicable.

3. The account numbers for all decedent's savings accounts, checking accounts, stocks, bonds and other investments.

4. The decedent's safe deposit box number and the location of the safe deposit box key.

5. The location and address of the decedent's banks and the name of the bank officer at each of the banks.

6. The account numbers for all of the decedent's credit card accounts.

7. The decedent's burial instructions and cemetery lot information.

8. Information concerning the decedent's life insurance policies and the location of the policies.

9. Information concerning any other insurance the decedent may have which could be used to indemnify the estate against any claims which may be brought against it, such as malpractice, homeowner and automobile insurance.

10. The location and description of personal property which may be in the possession of someone else, such as artwork on loan to a museum.

11. The names and addresses of persons who may have information concerning the decedent's financial affairs, such as his or her attorney, accountant, stockbroker, etc.

12. Information concerning past employment and pension, retirement or profit-sharing plan entitlements.

13. Personal documents, such as the decedent's birth certificate, death certificate, social security card, marriage certificate, divorce papers, passport, etc.

14. Complete and accurate tax records to enable the personal representative to better handle any claims made against the estate by the taxing authorities that might otherwise be inexplicable.

15. Records and books concerning any loans the decedent may have made, or debts he or she may have incurred in order to better enable

the personal representative to collect on monies payable to the estate and/or avoid paying out fraudulent claims against the estate.

16. The names and addresses of all heirs, legatees, devisees and next of kin.

17. Deeds and mortgage documents for any real property owned by the decedent.

18. Title and ownership documents to any vehicles owned by the decedent.

19. Social security records to assist in determining applicable benefits.

20. Military records to assist in determining applicable benefits.

APPRAISING THE ASSETS

The personal representative is responsible for having each estate item appraised so that the value of the estate can be determined. The court may require a court-appointed referee to determine the value of the property unless the appointment is waived by the court. Nevertheless, appraisal of general items may be undertaken by the personal representative with the assistance of certain valuation guides, such as the "blue book" for automobile valuation.

More unique items, such as jewelry or family heirlooms, may be appraised by a professional knowledgeable in the particular area. Real estate may be appraised by a real estate appraiser. The costs of professional appraisers may be paid out of the estate account.

CATEGORIZING ASSETS

Depending on the state, the inventory may include both probate and nonprobate assets.

Probate Assets

Probate assets generally consist of all of the decedent's real and personal property, including but not limited to homes, motor vehicles, bank accounts, household items, jewelry and personal effects. The personal representative should, on behalf of the estate, take possession of all probate assets of the estate. The letters of administration give the personal representative the authority to take possession of such assets and third parties are obligated to promptly transfer title or turn over the assets to the personal representative.

Nonprobate Assets

Nonprobate assets would include any jointly owned property, and property which names an individual beneficiary, such as life insurance proceeds, pension and certain trusts. Nonprobate assets pass directly to the named beneficiary or co-owner.

Jointly Owned Property

Any property held in joint tenancy by the decedent passes directly to the other joint tenants, each of whom is deemed to have an equal interest in the property. For example, married couples commonly hold deeds to marital real estate and bank accounts as joint tenants. However, some states have restricted or abolished joint tenancy, and jointly owned property that does not provide for a right of survivorship is generally deemed a probate asset to the extent of the portion owned by the decedent.

Another form of joint real estate ownership, available only to married couples, is tenancy by the entirety. This type of arrangement also avoids probate, since each of the spouses is considered to hold title to the whole property and the death of one spouse does not affect the other spouse's ownership of the whole property. Similar to a joint tenancy, a tenancy by the entirety is grounded in the common-law theory that a husband and wife are one person.

FINAL INVENTORY AND APPRAISAL

Within a prescribed time period, the personal representative is required to file a final inventory and appraisal of all the assets in the estate with the court. Copies of the final inventory and appraisal should also be sent to all interested parties.

A sample inventory and appraisal is set forth at Appendix 10.

OPENING AN ESTATE ACCOUNT

The personal representative is responsible for opening a bank account in the name of the estate. All income from the estate should be deposited in this account, and all costs of estate administration should be paid from this account. In addition, all of the decedent's existing bank accounts should be closed and the proceeds accounted for and deposited in the estate account.

The estate assets should always be kept separate from the personal funds of the personal representative. It is important that the personal representative maintain accurate financial records during administration of the estate. This will be helpful in preparing a final accounting of the estate for the court.

CHAPTER 5:
PROSECUTING AND DEFENDING
ESTATE CLAIMS

IN GENERAL

The personal representative is responsible for making sure that any claims that the estate may have against third parties are properly prosecuted, and any claims against the estate are properly defended.

PROSECUTING CLAIMS ON BEHALF OF THE ESTATE

If the decedent's estate has any claims against any third parties, the personal representative is responsible for seeing that the claim is pursued.

Tax Refunds

In some cases, the deceased may have overpaid federal or state taxes, thus the estate would be entitled to file for a refund. The personal representative is responsible for filing the appropriate refund application form.

A sample claim for a state tax refund on behalf of a deceased taxpayer is set forth at Appendix 11.

Wrongful Death Action

It is not uncommon for a personal representative to have to bring a wrongful death action on behalf of a decedent whose death was intentionally, negligently or recklessly caused by the wrongful conduct of another. Depending on state law, damages sought in the wrongful death action may include the value of the life of the decedent, pain and suffering, and medical and funeral expenses.

The personal representative is responsible for hiring an attorney to represent the decedent's claim and for collecting any monies which would be due the decedent's estate as a result of a settlement or judgment.

A sample petition to settle a wrongful death action on behalf of the decedent's estate is set forth at Appendix 12.

DEFENDING CLAIMS AGAINST THE ESTATE

The personal representative is responsible for seeing that any claims that are made against the decedent's estate, including debts and taxes that may be owed, are satisfied in a manner most advantageous to the estate.

Taxes

As more fully discussed in Chapter 6, the personal representative is responsible for making sure all taxes owed by the estate are paid. In determining what taxes must paid, the following steps must be taken:

1. The value of the estate and the estimated state and federal taxes must be computed.

2. A valuation date for federal estate tax must be selected.

3. A determination should be made as to whether administrative expenses should be charged against income taxes or estate taxes.

4. The final income tax return of the decedent must be prepared.

5. The estate income tax return must be prepared.

6. Deductions, including charitable deductions, must be determined.

7. A decision must be made as to how funds will be raised to pay taxes.

8. State inheritance tax returns must be prepared.

9. Federal inheritance tax returns must be prepared.

10. Personal property or real estate taxes must be paid.

Unpaid Bills

Most people die leaving behind a number of unpaid bills. Of course, medical and funeral bills often follow a death. There may be outstanding household bills and credit card debts. The personal representative generally collects all of the bills mailed to the decedent's home. Settling these debts is a part of estate administration. As set forth in Chapter 3, the publication of a notice in an approved newspaper also serves to inform the decedent's creditors of the opening of the estate.

To assist in determining and handling payment of the decedent's debts, the personal representative should:

1. Review current bills owed, including doctor, hospital, rent, utilities, etc.

2. Review the decedent's charge accounts statements.

3. Determine what loans exist, including mortgages, life insurance loans, bank loans, automobile loans, etc.

Presentation of Claims

Creditors are required to present their claims within a certain time period, after which all claims are barred. Most states require that creditors' claims be submitted to the court, however, some states allow the personal representative to accept the claims directly.

The personal representative is responsible for accumulating all of the claims, evaluating them and paying all valid claims. If the personal representative is not satisfied that a particular claim is valid, he or she will mail a notice of disallowance to the particular creditor. The notice may disallow all or part of the creditor's claim. The creditor must then respond within a certain time period after receiving the disallowance.

After the time period for submitting claims has expired, the personal representative will pay all valid claims, including taxes. Payment of large claims may require court approval. If the estate does not have enough assets to pay all of the claims, certain preferred claims must be paid before the rest of the assets are distributed. Preferred claims may include probate fees and funeral expenses.

The personal representative should obtain a receipt or voucher for every bill and claim paid and keep a record of all such payments to assist in preparing the final accounting.

Selling Assets

If the estate lacks liquid assets, the distributees may contribute cash into the estate account rather than suffer the forced sale of an asset. If the distributees do not contribute cash into the estate account, it may be necessary to sell certain estate assets to pay claims. For example, most estates include real property, the sale of which may be necessary to raise money for estate expenses or distribution.

The sale of real property entails all of the tasks normally associated with such a sale, including hiring professionals such as real estate brokers, appraisers and lawyers. Further, the personal representative must be familiar with the particular state's homestead exemption law which may prevent any sale while the property is occupied by a surviving spouse or children.

CHAPTER 6:
TAX ISSUES

IN GENERAL

An important aspect of probating an estate concerns the filing of tax returns and payment of any taxes owed. The tax returns are filed with the state or federal taxing authorities during estate administration. The taxes are paid out of the estate's assets.

TYPES OF TAX RETURNS

There are a number of tax returns which may have to be filed during administration of the decedent's estate. These may include the decedent's personal federal, state and/or local income tax returns; the estate federal and/or state income tax returns; the state inheritance or estate tax return; and the federal estate tax return.

A small estate may incur little or no tax consequences, thus, the returns will generally be simpler to complete than a larger estate. If the tax situation is particularly complex, the personal representative may require the assistance of a professional accountant in completing and filing the returns.

INCOME TAX

Decedent's Personal Income Tax

A decedent's income earned during the tax year in which he or she dies is subject to income tax to the extent the income exceeds the allowable deductions and exemptions. The personal representative is required to file a federal income tax return, and pay any taxes owed. A state income tax return may have to be filed as well.

Estate Income Tax

An estate may generate income from a number of sources during the period of administration, such as rental or interest income. The personal representative is required to file federal and state income tax returns on behalf of the decedent's estate to the extent the estate's income exceeds the appropriate exemptions for the tax year.

ESTATE TAX

The Federal Estate Tax

Federal estate tax, also known as death tax, is the tax imposed on the right to transfer property by death. Thus, the responsible party for paying estate tax is the decedent's estate, not the inheritors of the property. All property owned by the deceased may be subject to payment of federal estate taxes, whether or not the transfer avoids probate, including life insurance.

In 2003, the estate tax affects only people who die leaving a taxable estate of more than a million dollars. The estate tax threshold will continue to rise until 2010, when the tax will be repealed. The top tax rate will eventually drop to 45%. However, since the filing requirement is based on the gross estate, and does not take into account items such as the allowable exemptions, taxes will not necessarily be due and the fact is that most estates are never subject to tax.

To determine whether the estate will incur federal estate tax, one should first estimate the net worth of the property of the estate. Allowable exemptions may then be deducted, including: (1) the marital deduction, which provides an exemption for all property left to the surviving spouse; (2) the charitable organization exemption, which provides an exemption for all gifts made to a tax-exempt charity; and (3) the $1,000,000 threshold exemption. Keep in mind, however, that any taxable gifts made during the decedent's lifetime can reduce the exemption accordingly. One way to reduce these taxes is to give away property before one's death.

As set forth above, if the decedent was married, due to the marital deduction, estate tax will not likely be an issue until the second spouse dies because when the first spouse dies, everything passes to the surviving spouse tax-free.

Repeal of the Federal Estate Tax

Congress has recently passed legislation that will gradually repeal the estate tax by 2010. However, it is always possible that Congress will revive the tax during this time period, or decide not to renew the bill once it expires in 2011. Nevertheless, over the next 7 years, it is expected that rates will go down and exemptions will go up.

The federal gift tax has not been repealed, however, the lifetime gift tax exemption rose to $1 million dollars in 2002. That means an individual is able to make a total of $1 million of taxable gifts during their lifetime before owing any federal gift tax. In addition, an individual can make an unlimited number of $11,000 gifts, to different recipients, of cash or other property each calendar year, completely tax-free.

A table setting forth the new estate and gift tax rates is set forth at Appendix 13.

State Estate and Inheritance Tax

Estate Tax

States are also empowered to impose death taxes on their residents. State estate taxes are similar to the estate tax imposed by the federal government. The estate must pay this tax regardless of the relationship between the decedent and the beneficiaries.

Generally, such taxes are assessed on the resident's personal property and any real property located in the state. Most states had effectively abolished these taxes. In the rest, the state generally took a share of the money owed to the federal government. However, since federal legislation began to phase-out the federal estate tax, this reduced the share of estate tax that the states were entitled to keep. Thus, to compensate for this loss, some states are collecting tax from estates that aren't big enough to owe any federal tax.

States that presently impose a separate death tax include Connecticut (to be phased out by 2005); Indiana; Iowa; Kentucky; Louisiana (to be phased out by 2004); Maryland; Nebraska (county inheritance tax only); New Jersey; Ohio; Oklahoma; Pennsylvania; and Tennessee.

If the decedent maintained residences in more than one state, his or her domicile must be determined. The decedent's domicile is the state with which the decedent had the most significant ties, such as the state in which he or she voted, carried on his or her business, and owned his or her primary residence. Of course, it would be to the estate's benefit if the decedent's domicile is determined to be in the state that imposes little or no death taxes. Accordingly, people who maintain residences in more than one state may want to establish their domicile in the state that imposes little or no death taxes.

Inheritance Tax

Some states impose an inheritance tax, which is a tax on the inheritor's right to receive property from the estate. The inheritance tax is paid by the heirs, not by the estate. Typically, the amount the heirs pay depends on their relationship to the decedent. For example, a higher inheritance tax would be imposed on property left to a friend as opposed to a child. The rates vary from state to state, therefore, the reader is advised to check the law of his or her own jurisdiction for specific rate information.

CHAPTER 7:
DISTRIBUTING THE ASSETS AND CLOSING THE ESTATE

IN GENERAL

The personal representative is responsible for distributing the decedent's assets according to his or her wishes, or the estate's intestacy laws if the decedent died without a will. In general, those duties include:

1. Determining who is entitled to a share in the decedent's estate;

2. Selling estate assets to raise cash for specific legacies.

3. Determining how estate assets will be distributed, and which legatee and devisee is to get each item of property.

4, Paying all final costs, including any child support obligation.

5. Arranging for the transfer and reregister of securities.

6. Preparing a detailed informal or formal accounting for the court.

7. Obtaining releases and refunding bonds from all beneficiaries and filing documents with the Court.

TRANSFERRING PROPERTY OUTSIDE OF PROBATE

Most estates have assets which can be transferred directly to the beneficiaries—such as the heirs or the surviving spouse—or to one or more co-owners, without going through the probate process. Thus, transfer of these properties can be accomplished before the probate estate is closed. In addition, some states provide various exemptions from the probate process by either allowing a certain amount of the deceased's property to be completely exempt from probate or subject to a much more simplified probate process than normal.

A table of state statutes concerning state law exceptions to conventional probate is set forth at Appendix 3.

JOINTLY OWNED PROPERTY

Any property held in joint tenancy by the decedent passes directly to the other joint tenants, each of whom is deemed to have an equal interest in the property. Married couples commonly hold deeds to marital real estate and bank accounts as joint tenants. However, some states have restricted or abolished joint tenancy.

Another form of real estate ownership, available only to married couples, is tenancy by the entirety. This type of arrangement also avoids probate, since each of the spouses is considered to hold title to the whole property and the death of one spouse does not affect the other spouse's ownership of the whole property. Similar to a joint tenancy, a tenancy by the entirety is grounded in the common-law theory that a husband and wife are one person.

It must be determined whether assets which were co-owned by the decedent and one or more other individuals pass to the surviving co-owners. Some states deem all property owned by a married couple as containing a right of survivorship. Other states require the title to certain property to specifically state that there is a right of survivorship. The reader is advised to check the law of his or her own jurisdiction concerning specific requirements in this regard.

A right of survivorship generally means that the surviving owners of a certain piece of property automatically take title to the portion owned by the decedent upon his or her death. This form of ownership is generally referred to as joint tenancy. Some states require that the title specifically state that there is a right of survivorship.

Unless otherwise provided for in the ownership papers, each of the surviving co-owners would receive an equal share of the decedent's interest in the property. If there is only one surviving co-owner, he or she would become the owner of the whole property.

In order to accomplish the transfer of jointly owned property, the state may require documentation including but not limited to proof of the death of the decedent, such as a certified copy of the death certificate; and proof that the property was jointly owned and that the surviving co-owners have the right to the decedent's share of the property. The reader is advised to check the law of his or her own jurisdiction to determine the necessary forms which must be filed to effectuate the transfer.

Community Property States

There are eight community property states including Arizona, California, Idaho, Louisiana, Nevada, New Mexico, Texas and Washington. In community property states, all property and earnings acquired during the marriage, excluding gifts or inheritances, are deemed community property.

Community property does not include a right of survivorship, thus the surviving spouse does not automatically take ownership over the decedent's one-half share of the property. The decedent's share of the property is generally subject to the probate process, and must pass by will to the designated beneficiary, or according to the state's intestacy laws. Some community property states have special provisions eliminating the necessity for probate when the property will pass to the surviving spouse.

LIFE INSURANCE AND PENSION PLAN PROCEEDS

The proceeds from a life insurance policy, or pension plan, are not subject to probate, provided that the named beneficiary is not the decedent's estate. After the completion of certain required forms, the proceeds are paid directly to the named beneficiaries. If the named beneficiary is the decedent's estate, then the policy is subject to probate.

It is important to determine whether there are any additional sources of death benefits to which the decedent's heirs may be entitled, including social security benefits; veterans benefits; employee benefits, such as profit-sharing plans; union benefits; or benefits derived from other private retirement plans.

ASSET DISTRIBUTION

The remainder of the property left in the estate after payment of claims, expenses and taxes, is distributed according to the decedent's will, or according to the state intestacy laws, if there is no valid will. Some debts, such as liens on certain assets, like real estate or automobiles, are not paid from the estate, but are assumed by the inheritor of the particular asset.

Beneficiaries

The beneficiaries named in the decedent's will are those persons, or entities the decedent wishes to receive his or her assets upon death. A beneficiary may be a (i) primary; (ii) alternate; or (iii) residuary beneficiary.

The primary beneficiary is the decedent's first choice to receive a specified gift of property. An alternate beneficiary may be named to receive that specific property if the primary beneficiary predeceases the decedent, and the will was not amended to change the primary beneficiary.

The residuary beneficiary is the person or entity which receives the balance of the decedent's estate—the residuary estate—if any, after all of the specific gifts of property are made. If alternate beneficiaries are not named for any specific gift of property, and the primary beneficiary predeceases the decedent, that property also passes to the residuary beneficiary.

SURVIVORSHIP PERIODS

The will generally provides for a survivorship period—a specified period of time during which the beneficiary must survive the decedent in order to inherit under the will. If the primary beneficiary dies shortly after the decedent, and there is no established survivorship period, the property intended for the primary beneficiary will pass under the primary beneficiary's will, in which case it may end up in the hands of strangers to the decedent. If the will provides for a survivorship period, and the decedent's primary beneficiary dies within that time period, e.g. 60 days, the property will pass instead to the alternate or residuary beneficiary under the original decedent's will.

DISTRIBUTION IN KIND

If there is not enough cash in the estate to fulfill specific bequests left by the will, the personal representative may have to sell estate assets. However, if a forced sale of the assets is not cost effective, most states provide for distribution in kind.

Distribution in kind refers to the surrender of certain assets of the estate in place of cash value. For the purposes of distribution in kind, the asset is valued as of the date of distribution instead of the date of death. Nevertheless, if the heirs demand cash, the physical assets of the estate may have to be sold.

Further, if a residuary beneficiary requests that a specific asset remain in the estate, or if the current market value of the specific asset does not equal the cash bequest, distribution in kind is not permissible and the asset cannot be distributed in lieu of the cash bequest.

INTESTATE DISTRIBUTION

If the decedent did not leave a valid will, the estate assets must be distributed according to the state's laws of intestacy. The personal representative simply follows the provisions of the state's intestacy laws in distributing the property to the heirs.

A table of state rules of inheritance is set forth at Appendix 2.

MINORS

If the decedent leaves property to a minor child, any substantial gift must be supervised by an adult guardian who must be named in the will. In most cases, the decedent simply names his or her surviving spouse. If there is no surviving spouse, the person who has been designated as the personal guardian to take custody of the child may also act as the guardian for the child's property.

This adult guardian is obligated to use the money to provide for the needs of the child, and is required to regularly report to the court on how the money is being spent. In addition, the guardian generally needs permission from the court before investing the child's property. When the child reaches the age of majority, the guardianship relationship automatically ends and the child is entitled to receive the remainder of his or her property.

APPOINTING A GUARDIAN FOR MINOR CHILDREN

If the decedent had minor children when he or she died, the children are usually placed in, or remain in, the custody of their surviving parent. If both parents die simultaneously or if the one parent available to care for the children dies, the children must be placed in the custody of another responsible adult—a personal guardian.

The will usually names the person the decedent wishes to fulfill the role of guardian of his or her minor children. Although the decedent is free to name whoever he or she desires, the decedent's choice usually requires court approval unless, of course, it is the surviving parent. In most cases, the court will abide by the decedent's wishes, unless there is a question of the designated person's fitness or someone contests the designation. The will may also name an alternate person to act as guardian, in the event his or her first choice is unavailable, unwilling, or unable to serve at the time of the decedent's death.

CLOSING THE ESTATE

The personal representative is responsible for filing the forms necessary to close the estate and release him or her from any further responsibility. In order to close the estate, a final accounting may be required. In some states, the personal representative is not released from responsibility until all of the assets are distributed, and a final report is filed with the court.

The Final Accounting

The final accounting details the assets and expenses of the estate, including taxes, and the balance of the estate to be distributed. If administration of the estate is court supervised, the accounting must be filed with the court. If administration is unsupervised, the personal representative gives the final accounting to the heirs.

Assets

The final accounting must detail all assets of the estate, including those assets uncovered in the initial inventory of the estate, and any assets recovered during estate administration.

Expenses

The final accounting must detail all estate expenses, including all of the decedent's bills and outstanding obligations at the time of death; burial expenses; fees for the personal representative and other professionals hired by the estate during administration; and any ongoing estate expenses.

Taxes

After deducting the expenses from the assets, the applicable taxes must be calculated on the estate balance less any exemptions.

Balance of Estate

After payment of the taxes, the balance of the estate is distributed to the decedent's beneficiaries and/or heirs. The final accounting should include the intended distribution, with a detailed list of the assets to be distributed and the recipients.

The Supervised Estate

Court supervised estate administration requires that the final accounting be filed with the court. The accounting should include copies of all applicable receipts and proof of payment, such as canceled checks. An audit may be conducted to confirm the accuracy of the accounting figures. Following the audit, the estate may be formally closed. Generally, this may be accomplished either by petition to the court, or by sworn statement.

Court Petition

If closing is sought by court petition, the personal representative must submit the final accounting to the court with the petition. After the court has reviewed the petition, it sets a hearing date. Notice of the hearing date must be sent to all interested persons, including any creditors of the estate. At the final hearing, the court may resolve any outstanding issues, such as a fee reduction request. After all issues have been resolved, the court approves the final accounting and proposed distribution of the estate, and orders that distribution proceed.

Sworn Statement

If closing is sought by sworn statement, the personal representative must submit a form to the court which details, under oath, all of the steps which were taken in administering the estate. Copies of the final accounting and sworn statement must be distributed to all interested persons.

A sample petition for judicial settlement of an estate is set forth at Appendix 14.

Once the estate has been fully administered, all assets of the estate have been distributed, and the final accounting and required exhibits have been filed, the court will issue a final order discharging the personal representative from all further duties and responsibilities.

A sample order of final discharge is set forth at Appendix 15.

CHAPTER 8:
GOVERNMENT BENEFITS

IN GENERAL

One of the tasks the personal representative may undertake is to determine whether the decedent's survivors are entitled to any type of government benefit. If the decedent served in the armed forces, the decedent's estate is eligible for many burial-related benefits. These benefits are not automatic and must be applied for within a certain time period. It is the personal representative's responsibility to determine such benefits, as they may be a factor in the decedent's burial arrangements.

In addition, the decedent's Social Security records must be examined to determine whether the decedent earned enough work credits so that the decedent's survivors are eligible for benefits.

VETERAN'S BENEFITS

A veteran of the armed services is entitled to many burial-related benefits. However, these benefits are not paid automatically. In general, claims for veteran's benefits must be made within two years from the date of final interment.

As an honorably discharged veteran or member of the Armed Services, including the Air Force, Army, Navy, Marines, or Coast Guard, the decedent's estate may be entitled to the following burial-related benefits:

1. A burial allowance limited to $300.00 for expenses for burial and funeral of the deceased. This allowance will be paid only for veterans who were entitled to receive a Veterans Administration pension or compensation.

2. Burial at a gravesite in any of the Veteran's Administration's 120 national cemeteries, including the opening and closing of the grave, and perpetual care.

3. A burial flag that can be given to next of kin or friend of the deceased veteran.

4. A bronze memorial or headstone.

5. A Presidential Memorial Certificate.

6. An allowance of $150.00 payable towards the burial plot expenses of a veteran who is not buried in a national cemetery. However, this allowance will be paid only for veterans who were entitled to receive a Veterans Administration pension or compensation.

Filing a Claim

The deceased veteran's personal representative, or other person making the burial arrangements, should have the funeral home contact the national cemetery in which burial is desired, in order to schedule the burial. The following information concerning the deceased veteran should be provided when the cemetery is contacted:

1. Full name and military rank.

2. Branch of service.

3. Social security number.

4. Service number.

5. VA claim number, if applicable.

6. Date and place of birth.

7. Date and place of death.

8. Date of retirement or last separation from active duty.

In addition, the following documents will be required when filing a claim:

1. A copy of any military separation documents, such as the Department of Defense Form 214 (DD-214).The veteran's discharge papers must specify active military duty and show that release from active duty was under other than dishonorable conditions.

2. A certified copy of the veteran's death certificate.

3. An itemized funeral bill with a paid receipt.

To determine the deceased veteran's eligibility for burial-related benefits, or to file a claim on behalf of the decedent's estate, contact the Department of Veterans Affairs, 810 Vermont Avenue, NW, Washington, DC 20402 or call (202) 872-1151.

Eligible Persons

Eligibility for burial-related benefits includes those in the following categories:

Veterans and Members of the Armed Forces

Veterans and members of the Armed Forces, including the Army, Navy, Air Force, Marine Corps and Coast Guard, as follows:

1. Any member of the Armed Forces of the United States who dies on active duty.

2. Any veteran who was discharged under conditions other than dishonorable. With certain exceptions, service beginning after September 7, 1980, as an enlisted person, and service after October 16, 1981, as an officer, must be for a minimum of 24 months or the full period for which the person was called to active duty. Undesirable, bad conduct, and any other type of discharge other than honorable may or may not qualify the individual for veterans benefits, depending upon a determination made by the Veteran's Administration.

3. Any citizen of the United States who, during any war in which the United States has been or may hereafter be engaged, served in the Armed Forces of any Government allied with the United States during that war, whose last active service was terminated honorably by death or otherwise, and who was a citizen of the United States at the time of entry into such service and at the time of death.

Members of Reserve Components and Reserve Officers' Training Corps

Members of Reserve Components and Reserve Officers' Training Corps, as follows:

1. Reservists and National Guard members who, at the time of their death, were entitled to retired pay under Chapter 1223, title 10, United States Code, or would have been entitled, but for being under the age of 60. Specific categories of individuals eligible for retired pay are delineated in section 12731 of Chapter 1223, title 10, United States Code.

2. Members of reserve components who die while hospitalized or undergoing treatment at the expense of the United States for injury or disease contracted or incurred under honorable conditions while performing active duty for training or inactive duty training, or undergoing such hospitalization or treatment.

3. Members of the Reserve Officers' Training Corps of the Army, Navy, or Air Force who die under honorable conditions while attending an authorized training camp or on an authorized cruise, while performing authorized travel to or from that camp or cruise, or while hospitalized or undergoing treatment at the expense of the United States for injury or disease contracted or incurred under honorable conditions while engaged in one of those activities.

4. Members of reserve components who, during a period of active duty for training, were disabled or died from a disease or injury incurred or aggravated in line of duty or, during a period of inactive duty training, were disabled or died from an injury incurred or aggravated in line of duty.

Commissioned Officers of the National Oceanic and Atmospheric Administration

Commissioned Officers of the National Oceanic and Atmospheric Administration, as follows:

1. A Commissioned Officer of the National Oceanic and Atmospheric Administration, formerly the Coast and Geodetic Survey and the Environmental Science Services Administration, with full-time duty on or after July 29, 1945.

2. A Commissioned Officer who served before July 29, 1945, and;

(a) Was assigned to an area of immediate military hazard while in time of war, or of a Presidentially declared national emergency as determined by the Secretary of Defense;

(b) Served in the Philippine Islands on December 7, 1941, and continuously in such islands thereafter; or,

(c) Transferred to the Department of the Army or the Department of the Navy under the provisions of the Act of May 22, 1917 (40 Stat. 87; 33 U.S.C. § 855).

Officers of the Public Health Service

Officers of the Public Health Service, including:

1. A Commissioned Officer of the Regular or Reserve Corps of the Public Health Service who served on full-time duty on or after July 29, 1945. If the service of the particular Public Health Service Officer falls within the meaning of active duty for training, as defined in section 101(22), title 38, United States Code, he or she must have been disabled or died from a disease or injury incurred or aggravated in the line of duty.

2. A Commissioned Officer of the Regular or Reserve Corps of the Public Health Service who performed full-time duty prior to July 29, 1945:

(a) In time of war;

(b) On detail for duty with the Army, Navy, Air Force, Marine Corps, or Coast Guard; or,

(c) While the Service was part of the military forces of the United States pursuant to Executive Order of the President.

3. A Commissioned Officer serving on inactive duty training as defined in section 101(23), title 38, United States Code, whose death resulted from an injury incurred or aggravated in the line of duty.

World War II Merchant Mariners

World War II Merchant Mariners, as follows:

1. United States Merchant Mariners with oceangoing service during the period of armed conflict, December 7, 1941, to December 31, 1946. Prior to the enactment of Public Law 105-368, United States Merchant Mariners with oceangoing service during the period of armed conflict of December 7, 1941, to August 15, 1945, were eligible. With enactment of Public Law 105-368, the service period is extended to December 31, 1946, for those dying on or after November 11, 1998, provided the Mariner's death occurred after the enactment of the law.

2. United States Merchant Mariners who served on blockships in support of Operation Mulberry during World War II.

Spouses and Dependents

Spouses and dependents of eligible persons, as follows:

1. The spouse or unremarried surviving spouse of an eligible person, even if that person is not buried or memorialized in a national cemetery, is eligible for interment in a national cemetery. In addition, the spouse of a member of the Armed Forces of the United States lost or buried at sea, or officially determined to be permanently absent in a status of missing or missing in action, or whose remains have been donated to science or cremated and the ashes scattered is also eligible for burial.

2. The surviving spouse of an eligible decedent who remarries an ineligible individual and whose remarriage is void, terminated by the ineligible individual's death, or dissolved by annulment or divorce is

eligible for burial in a national cemetery. The surviving spouse of an eligible decedent who remarries an eligible person retains his or her eligibility for burial in a national cemetery.

3. The minor children of an eligible person. For purpose of burial in a national cemetery, a minor child is a person who is unmarried and:

(a) Who is under the age of 21 years; or,

(b) Who is under 23 years of age and pursuing a course of instruction at an approved educational institution.

4. An unmarried adult child of an eligible person if the child is physically or mentally disabled and incapable of self-support before reaching the age of 21 years.

Other Persons

Such other persons or classes of persons as designated by the Secretary of Veterans Affairs (38 U.S.C. § 2402(6)) or the Secretary of the Air Force (Public Law 95-202, § 401), or (38 CFR § 3.7(x)), may be eligible.

Ineligible Persons

The following persons are not eligible for burial in a Veterans Administration National Cemetery:

1. A surviving spouse of an eligible decedent who marries an ineligible individual and predeceases that individual.

2. A former spouse of an eligible individual whose marriage to that individual has been terminated by annulment or divorce, if not otherwise eligible.

3. Family members of an eligible person.

4. A person whose only separation from the Armed Forces was under dishonorable conditions or whose character of service results in a bar to veterans benefits.

5. A person who was ordered to report to an induction station, but was not actually inducted into military service.

6. Pursuant to 38 U.S.C. § 2411:

(a) a person found guilty of a Federal capital crime and sentenced to death or life imprisonment;

(b) a person convicted of a State capital crime, and sentenced to death or life imprisonment without parole; or

(c) a person who is shown by clear and convincing evidence to have committed a Federal or State capital crime but was not convicted of such crime because of flight to avoid prosecution or by death prior to trial.

7. Any person convicted of subversive activities after September 1, 1959, unless the President has granted a pardon.

8. A person whose only service is active duty for training or inactive duty training in the National Guard or Reserve Component, unless the individual meets certain eligibility criteria.

9. Members of groups whose service has been determined by the Secretary of the Air Force under the provisions of Public Law 95-202 as not warranting entitlement to benefits administered by the Secretary of Veterans Affairs.

An application for VA death benefits is set forth at Appendix 16.

SOCIAL SECURITY BENEFITS

When a person who has worked and paid Social Security taxes dies, certain members of the family may be eligible for survivor's benefits if the decedent earned enough work credits prior to their death. A portion of the Social Security taxes one pays is applied to this survivor's insurance. In addition, a lump sum death benefit is also payable at that time.

An individual can earn up to a maximum of four credits each year. Presently, one work credit is equal to $890 of wages or self-employment income. Therefore, once an individual has earned $3,560, they have earned their four credits for the year.

The number of credits needed to provide survivor benefits depends on the decedent's age when they die. The younger a person is, the fewer credits he or she must have for family members to receive survivor's benefits. But no one needs more than 40 credits, equal to 10 years of work, to be eligible for any Social Security benefit.

Nevertheless, benefits can be paid to the decedent's children, and their spouse who is caring for the children, even if the decedent didn't earn the required number of credits. In that case, the decedent's survivors can get benefits if the decedent earned credit for one and one-half years of work, equal to 6 credits, in the three years prior to their death.

Eligible Survivors

Social Security survivors benefits can be paid to the following family members of the decedent:

Widow/Widower

Full survivor's benefits are payable to the decedent's widow or widower at full retirement age, which is currently age 65, or reduced benefits as early as age 60. A disabled widow or widower is eligible for benefits as early as age 50. In addition, the widow or widower may be eligible for benefits at any age where he or she takes care of the decedent's child, if the child is under the age of 16 or disabled and receiving Social Security benefits.

Unmarried Children

Unmarried children under age 18 are entitled to survivor's benefits. The benefits may extend to age 19 if the child is still attending high school full-time. In some cases, stepchildren, grandchildren or adopted children are also eligible for benefits. In addition, disabled children of any age may be eligible for benefits provided the disability occurred before age 22 and the child remains disabled.

Parents

Parents who were dependent on the decedent, and who are age 62 or older, are eligible for survivor's benefits.

Divorce and Remarriage

If a divorced spouse dies, the surviving divorced spouse may also receive benefits as a widow or widower if the marriage lasted 10 years or longer. In addition, benefits paid to a surviving divorced spouse who is 60 or older will not affect the benefit rates for other survivors who are receiving benefits.

However, the surviving divorced spouse cannot receive survivor's benefits if he or she remarries before the age of 60, unless the second marriage ends, whether by death, divorce, or annulment. If the surviving divorced spouse remarries after age 60, or 50 if disabled, he or she can still collect benefits on their former spouse's record. When the surviving divorced spouse reaches age 62 or older, he or she may get retirement benefits on the record of their new spouse if they are higher. Nevertheless, the surviving divorced spouse's remarriage would have no effect on the benefits being paid to the children.

Retirement

If a person is collecting survivor's benefits, he or she can switch to their own retirement benefits as early as age 62, assuming they are eligible and their retirement rate is higher than the widow/widower's rate. In most cases, one can begin receiving retirement benefits either on their own or their spouse's record at age 62, and then switch to the other benefit when they reach full retirement age, if that amount is higher.

Applying for Benefits

Application for social security survivor's benefits may be made by telephone or in person. In general, the following documentation may be required:

1. Proof of death from the funeral home, or an original or certified copy of the decedent's death certificate.

2. The decedent's social security number.

3. The applicant's social security number.

4. An original or certified copy of the applicant's birth certificate.

5. An original or certified copy of the applicant's marriage certificate if they are applying for widow or widower's benefits.

6. Proof of U.S. citizenship or lawful alien status if the applicant was born outside the United States.

7. An original or certified copy of the applicant's divorce papers if they are applying as a surviving divorced spouse.

8. The social security numbers of any dependent children.

9. The decedent's most recent W-4 forms or federal self-employment tax return.

10. The name of the applicant's bank and their account number so their benefits can be directly deposited into their account.

The Lump Sum Death Benefit

A lump sum death benefit will be made to the surviving spouse if he or she was living in the same household with the decedent at the time of death. If no qualified spouse survives, the payment can be made only to eligible children.

When applying for the lump sum death benefit, the applicant must provide the following additional information:

1. The applicant's name and social security number.

2. The decedent's name, gender, date of birth and social security number.

3. The decedent's date and place of death.

4. Information as to whether the decedent ever filed for Social Security benefits, Medicare or Supplemental Security Income.

5. Information as to whether the decedent was unable to work because of illnesses, injuries or conditions at any time during the 14 months prior to his or her death.

6. Information as to whether the decedent was ever in the active military service.

7. Information as to whether the decedent worked for the railroad industry for 7 years or more.

8. Information as to whether the decedent earned social security credits under another country's social security system.

9. The names, dates of birth, and social security numbers of any of the decedent's former spouses, and the dates of those marriages and how and when they ended.

10. The names of any of the decedent's unmarried children under 18, or up to 19 if still in secondary school, or any age if disabled prior to age 22 and still disabled.

11. The amount of the decedent's earnings in the year of death and the preceding year.

12. Information as to whether the decedent had a parent who was dependent on the worker for one-half of his or her support at the time of the worker's death.

13. Information as to whether the decedent and surviving spouse were living together at the time of death.

The surviving spouse will also be asked:

1. Whether they have been unable to work because of illness or injury at any time within the past 14 months.

2. Whether they, or anyone else, ever filed for Social Security benefits, Medicare or Supplemental Security Income on their own behalf.

3. The names, dates of birth, and social security numbers of any of the applicant's former spouses, the dates of those marriages, and how and when they ended.

Payments to Decedent After Death

If the decedent receives a check from Social Security for the month following the month of their death, it must be returned to the Social Security Administration. If the decedent received benefits by direct deposit into their bank account, the Social Security Administration will electronically take the payment back. If the surviving spouse also receives Social Security, the survivor will receive the higher amount of the two checks, but only one payment.

APPENDIX 1:
UNIFORM PROBATE CODE—
TABLE OF CONTENTS

PART 4 FORMAL TESTACY AND APPOINTMENT PROCEEDINGS

PART 10 CLOSING ESTATES

PART 5 POWERS OF ATTORNEY

APPENDIX 2:
STATE RULES OF INHERITANCE

STATE	APPLICABLE STATUTE	BASIC INHERITANCE RULES
Alabama	Alabama Code, Title 43, §§43-1-1 et. seq.	100% to surviving spouse if no surviving children or parents; $50,000 plus 1/2 of estate to surviving spouse if surviving children and all are issue of surviving spouse; 1/2 of estate to surviving spouse if surviving children and all not issue of surviving spouse; $100,000 plus 1/2 of estate to surviving spouse if surviving parents but no surviving children.
Alaska	Alaska Statutes, §13.11.005	100% to surviving spouse if no surviving children or parents; $50,000 plus 1/2 of estate to surviving spouse if surviving children and all issue of surviving spouse; 1/2 of estate to surviving spouse if surviving children and all not issue of surviving spouse; $50,000 plus 1/2 of estate to surviving spouse if surviving parents but no children.
Arizona	Arizona Revised Statutes, §§14-2101 et. seq.	1/2 of all community property to surviving spouse; 100% of community property and separate property to surviving spouse if no surviving children or if surviving children and all are issue of surviving spouse; 1/2 of all community property and 1/2 of all separate property to surviving spouse if surviving children and all not issue of surviving spouse.

STATE	APPLICABLE STATUTE	BASIC INHERITANCE RULES
Arkansas	Arkansas Statutes Annotated, §§28-8-101 et. seq.	Entire estate to surviving children or descendants of deceased children; if no such descendants then 100% to surviving spouse if married for 3 years; if not married for 3 years then 50% to surviving spouse and 50% to surviving parents; if no surviving children or spouse then 100% to surviving parents.
California	California Probate Code, §§1 et. seq.	1/2 of all community property and 1/2 of all decedent's community property to surviving spouse; 100% of all separate property to surviving spouse if no surviving children parents siblings or issue of siblings; 1/2 of separate property to surviving spouse if one surviving child, issue of deceased child, surviving parent or issue of parent; 1/3 of separate property if more than one surviving child or issue of two or more deceased children.
Colorado	Colorado Revised Statutes, §§15-1-101 et. seq.	100% to surviving spouse if no surviving children; $25,000 plus 1/2 of estate to surviving spouse if surviving children and all are issue of surviving spouse; 1/2 of estate to surviving spouse if surviving children and all not issue of surviving spouse.

STATE	APPLICABLE STATUTE	BASIC INHERITANCE RULES
Connecticut	Connecticut General Statutes Annotated, §§45-1 et. seq.	100% to surviving spouse if no surviving children, issue of deceased children, or surviving parents; $100,000 plus 1/2 of estate to surviving spouse if surviving children and all are issue of surviving spouse; 1/2 of estate to surviving spouse if surviving children and all not issue of surviving spouse; $100,000 plus 3/4 of estate to surviving spouse if surviving parents but no surviving children; if no surviving children or spouse 100% to surviving parents.
Delaware	Delaware Code Annotated, Title 12, §§101 et. seq.	100% to surviving spouse if no surviving children or parents; $50,000 plus 1/2 of personal estate and life estate in realty to surviving spouse if surviving children and all are issue of surviving spouse; 1/2 of personal estate and life estate in realty to surviving spouse if surviving children and all not issue of surviving spouse; $50,000 plus 1/2 of personal estate and life estate in realty to surviving spouse if surviving parent.
District of Columbia	District of Columbia Code, §§18-101 et. seq.	100% to surviving spouse if no surviving children, parents, grandchildren, siblings or children of siblings; 1/3 of estate to surviving spouse if surviving children or descendants of children; 1/2 of estate to surviving spouse if surviving parents, siblings or children of siblings, but no surviving children.

STATE	APPLICABLE STATUTE	BASIC INHERITANCE RULES
Florida	Florida Statutes Annotated, §§731.005 et. seq.	100% to surviving spouse if no surviving lineal descendants; $20,000 plus 1/2 of estate to surviving spouse if surviving children; 1/2 of estate to surviving spouse if decedent survived by a lineal descendant who is not a lineal descendant of surviving spouse.
Georgia	Georgia Statutes, Title 53, §§53-1-1 et. seq.	100% to surviving spouse if no surviving children or their descendants; child's share to surviving spouse if surviving children or their descendants; 1/5 to surviving spouse if more than five surviving children or their descendants except surviving husband always takes a child's share.
Hawaii	Hawaii Revised Statutes, §§560 et. seq.	100% to surviving spouse if no surviving children or parents; 1/2 of estate to surviving spouse if surviving children or parent.
Idaho	Idaho Code, §§15-1-101 et. seq.	1/2 of community property to surviving spouse with balance distributed to decedent's surviving descendants according to statute; 100% of separate property estate to surviving spouse if no surviving children or parents; $50,000 plus 1/2 of separate property estate to surviving spouse if surviving children and all are issue of surviving spouse; 1/2 of separate property estate to surviving spouse if surviving children and all not issue of surviving spouse; $50,000 plus 1/2 of separate property estate to surviving spouse if surviving parents but no surviving children.

STATE	APPLICABLE STATUTE	BASIC INHERITANCE RULES
Illinois	Illinois Annotated Statutes, Chapter 110, §§1-1 et. seq.	100% to surviving spouse if no surviving descendants; 1/2 of estate to surviving spouse if surviving descendants; 100% to surviving descendants if no spouse; if no surviving spouse or descendants then entire estate to surviving parents, siblings or descendants of siblings in equal share except if there is only one surviving parent he or she takes both parents share.
Indiana	Indiana Statutes Annotated, §§29-1-1 et. seq.	100% to surviving spouse if no surviving children, descendants of children, or parents; 1/2 of estate to surviving spouse if surviving children or descendants of children.
Iowa	Iowa Code Annotated, §§633.1 et. seq.	If no surviving children surviving spouse receives 1/2 of real property, 100% of exempt personal property, and 1/2 of personal property after debts, but all must equal at least $50,000; if surviving children, surviving spouse receives 1/3 of real property, 100% of exempt personal property, and 1/2 of personal property after debts, but all must equal at least $50,000.
Kansas	Kansas Statutes Annotated, §§59-101	100% to surviving spouse if no surviving children or issue of deceased children; 1/2 of estate to surviving spouse if surviving children or issue of deceased children; if no surviving children, issue of deceased children or surviving spouse, 100% to surviving parents.

STATE	APPLICABLE STATUTE	BASIC INHERITANCE RULES
Kentucky	Kentucky Revised Statutes, §§391.010 et. seq.	100% to surviving spouse if no surviving children, issue of deceased children, surviving parents or siblings; 1/2 of personal property, fee estate in 1/2 of real estate and life estate in real estate to surviving spouse if surviving children, issue of deceased children, surviving parents or siblings; $7,500.00 to surviving spouse or surviving infant child.
Louisiana	Louisiana Civil Code Annotated, Article 1470 et. seq.	100% of community property if no surviving direct descendants; 1/2 of community property to surviving spouse if any surviving direct descendants.
Maine	Maine Revised Statutes Annotated, Title 18A, §§1-101 et. seq.	100% to surviving spouse if no surviving children or parents; $50,000 plus 1/2 of estate to surviving spouse if surviving children and all are issue of surviving spouse; 1/2 of estate to surviving spouse if surviving children and all not issue of surviving spouse; $50,000 plus 1/2 of estate to surviving spouse if surviving parents but no surviving children.
Maryland	Annotated Code of Maryland, Estates and Trusts Section	100% to surviving spouse if no surviving children or parents; $15,000 plus 1/2 of estate to surviving spouse if surviving children; 1/2 of estate to surviving spouse if surviving minor children; $15,000 plus 1/2 of estate to surviving spouse if surviving parents but no surviving children.

STATE	APPLICABLE STATUTE	BASIC INHERITANCE RULES
Massachusetts	Massachusetts General Laws Annotated, Chapter 190, §§1 et. seq.	100% to surviving spouse if no surviving children and estate does not exceed $50,000; if the estate exceeds $50,000 then $50,000 plus 1/2 of estate to surviving spouse; 1/2 of personal and real property to surviving spouse if surviving children.
Michigan	Michigan Comp. Laws Annotated, §§700.1 et. seq.	100% to surviving spouse if no surviving children or parents; $60,000 plus 1/2 of estate to surviving spouse if surviving children and all are issue of surviving spouse; 1/2 of estate to surviving spouse if surviving children and all not issue of surviving spouse; $60,000 plus 1/2 of estate to surviving spouse if surviving parent and no surviving children.
Minnesota	Minnesota Statutes Annotated, Chapters 524; 525 and 527	100% to surviving spouse if no surviving children; $70,000 plus 1/2 of estate to surviving spouse if surviving children and all are issue of surviving spouse; 1/2 of estate to surviving spouse if surviving children and all not issue of surviving spouse.
Mississippi	Mississippi Code Annotated, §§91-1-1 et. seq.	100% to surviving spouse if no surviving children or their descendants; if surviving children or their descendants, surviving spouse receives a child's share; children take in equal parts.

STATE	APPLICABLE STATUTE	BASIC INHERITANCE RULES
Missouri	Missouri Statutes Annotated, §§474.010 et. seq.	100% to surviving spouse if no surviving children or parents; $20,000 plus 1/2 of estate to surviving spouse if surviving children and all are issue of surviving spouse; 1/2 of estate to surviving spouse if surviving children and all not issue of surviving spouse; $20,000 plus 1/2 of estate to surviving spouse if surviving parents but no surviving children.
Montana	Montana Code Annotated, §§72-2-202 et. seq.	100% to surviving spouse if no surviving children or if all surviving children are issue of surviving spouse; 1/2 of estate to surviving spouse if one surviving child not the issue of surviving spouse; 1/3 of estate to surviving spouse if more than one surviving child not the issue of surviving spouse.
Nebraska	Revised Statutes of Nebraska, §§30-101 et. seq.	100% to surviving spouse if no surviving children or parents; $50,000 plus 1/2 of estate to surviving spouse if surviving children and all are issue of surviving spouse; 1/2 of estate to surviving spouse if surviving children and all not issue of surviving spouse; $50,000 plus 1/2 of estate to surviving spouse if surviving parents but no surviving children.

STATE	APPLICABLE STATUTE	BASIC INHERITANCE RULES
Nevada	Nevada Revised Statutes, Title 12, §§133.010 et. seq.	100% of community property to surviving spouse; 1/2 of separate property to surviving spouse if one surviving child or child's descendants; 1/3 of separate property to surviving spouse if more than one surviving child or their descendants; 1/2 of separate property to surviving spouse if surviving parents but no surviving children or their descendants; 1/2 of separate property to surviving spouse if surviving siblings but no surviving children or their descendants, or surviving parents.
New Hampshire	New Hampshire Revised Statutes Annotated, Chapter 551.1 et. seq.	100% to surviving spouse if no surviving children or parents; $50,000 plus 1/2 of estate to surviving spouse if surviving children and all are issue of surviving spouse; 1/2 of estate to surviving spouse if surviving children and all not issue of surviving spouse; $50,000 plus 1/2 of estate to surviving spouse if surviving parents but no surviving children.
New Jersey	Section 3B:3-1 et. seq., of the New Jersey Statutes Annotated, §§3B: 3-1 et. seq.	100% to surviving spouse if no surviving children or parents; $50,000 plus 1/2 of estate to surviving spouse if surviving children and all are issue of surviving spouse; 1/2 of estate to surviving spouse if surviving children and all not issue of surviving spouse; $50,000 plus 1/2 of estate to surviving spouse if surviving parents but no surviving children.
New Mexico	New Mexico Statutes Annotated, §§45-1-101 et. seq.	100% to surviving spouse if no surviving children; 100% of community property and 1/4 of separate property to surviving spouse if surviving children.

STATE	APPLICABLE STATUTE	BASIC INHERITANCE RULES
New York	Consolidated Laws of New York Annotated, EPTL §§1-1.1 et. seq.	$4,000 of personal property plus 1/2 of remaining personal property to surviving spouse if one surviving child or issue of deceased child; $4,000 of personal property plus 1/3 of remaining personal property to surviving spouse if more than one surviving child; $25,000 plus 1/2 of estate to surviving spouse if surviving parents but no surviving children.
North Carolina	General Statutes of North Carolina, §§28-A-1 et. seq.	100% to surviving spouse if no surviving children or their descendants, or surviving parents; 1/2 of all real property and first $15,000 of personal property plus 1/2 of balance of personal property to surviving spouse if one surviving child or descendant of child; 1/3 of all real property and first $15,000 of personal property plus 1/3 of balance of personal property if surviving children or descendants of children; 1/2 of real property and first $15,000 of personal property plus 1/2 of balance of personal property if surviving parents but no surviving children or descendants of children.
North Dakota	North Dakota Code, §§30.1-08-01 et. seq.	100% to surviving spouse if no surviving children or parents; $50,000 plus 1/2 of estate to surviving spouse if surviving children and all are issue of surviving spouse; 1/2 of estate to surviving spouse if surviving children and all not issue of surviving spouse; $50,000 plus 1/2 of estate to surviving spouse if surviving parents but no surviving children.

STATE	APPLICABLE STATUTE	BASIC INHERITANCE RULES
Ohio	Ohio Revised Code Annotated, §§2105 et. seq.	$60,000 plus 1/2 of estate to surviving spouse if one surviving child or descendant of deceased child, if child is issue of surviving spouse; $20,000 plus 1/2 of estate to surviving spouse if one surviving child or descendant of deceased child, if child is not issue of surviving spouse; $60,000 plus 1/3 of estate to surviving spouse if surviving children or descendants of deceased children, and all are issue of surviving spouse; $20,000 plus 1/3 of estate to surviving spouse if surviving children or descendants of children, and all are not issue of surviving spouse.
Oklahoma	Oklahoma Statutes Annotated, Title 84, §1-308	100% to surviving spouse if no surviving children, parents or siblings; 100% of joint property plus 1/3 of balance of estate if surviving parents or siblings but no surviving children; 1/2 of joint property and child's share of balance of estate if surviving children or descendants of children and all not issue of surviving spouse.
Oregon	Oregon Revised Statutes, §§112.015 et. seq.	100% to surviving spouse if no surviving children; 1/2 of estate to surviving spouse if surviving children.

STATE	APPLICABLE STATUTE	BASIC INHERITANCE RULES
Pennsylvania	Pennsylvania Statutes Annotated, Title 20, §§101 et. seq.	100% to surviving spouse if no surviving children or parents; $30,000 plus 1/2 of estate to surviving spouse if surviving children and all are issue of surviving spouse; 1/2 of estate to surviving spouse if surviving children and all not issue of surviving spouse; $30,000 plus 1/2 of estate to surviving spouse if surviving parents but no surviving children.
Rhode Island	General Laws of Rhode Island, §§33-1-1 et. seq.	All real property to surviving spouse for life subject to any encumbrances; 100% of entire estate to surviving spouse if no surviving children or kindred; $50,000 plus 1/2 of personal property to surviving spouse if surviving kindred but no surviving children; 1/2 of personal property to surviving spouse if surviving children.
South Carolina	Code of Laws of South Carolina, §§21-1-10 et. seq.	100% to surviving spouse if no surviving children or their descendants, parents, or siblings; 1/2 of estate to surviving spouse if one surviving child; 1/3 of estate to surviving spouse if more than one surviving child.
South Dakota	South Dakota Comp. Laws Annotated, §§29-1-1 et. seq.	1/2 of estate to surviving spouse if one surviving child or descendant of deceased child; 1/3 of estate to surviving spouse if more than one surviving child, or one surviving child and surviving descendants of deceased children; 100% of estate to surviving children or descendants of deceased children if no surviving spouse; $100,000 plus 1/2 of balance of estate to surviving spouse if surviving parents, siblings or descendants of siblings, but no surviving children.

STATE	APPLICABLE STATUTE	BASIC INHERITANCE RULES
Tennessee	Tennessee Code Annotated, §§30-101 et. seq.	100% to surviving spouse if no surviving children or their descendants; child's share not less than 1/3 of estate to surviving spouse if surviving children or their descendants.
Texas	Texas Probate Code, §§1 et. seq.	100% of community property to surviving spouse if no surviving children or their descendants; 1/2 of community property to surviving spouse if surviving children or their descendants; 100% of personal property and 1/2 of real property to surviving spouse if no surviving children or their descendants with balance to decedent's other surviving relatives; 1/3 of personal property and a life estate in 1/3 of real property to surviving spouse if surviving children or their descendants.
Utah	Utah Code, §§75-1-101 et. seq.	100% to surviving spouse if no surviving children or parents; $50,000 plus 1/2 of estate to surviving spouse if surviving children and all are issue of surviving spouse; 1/2 of estate to surviving spouse if surviving children and all not issue of surviving spouse; $100,000 plus 1/2 of estate to surviving spouse if surviving parents but no surviving children.
Vermont	Vermont Statutes Annotated, Title 14, §§1 et. seq.	Surviving spouse takes dower or curtesy equal to 1/3 of real property; if no surviving children, surviving spouse inherits $25,000 plus 1/2 of remainder; if decedent leaves no surviving kindred, surviving spouse inherits the entire estate; if decedent leaves surviving children, surviving spouse's share limited to dower or curtesy.

STATE	APPLICABLE STATUTE	BASIC INHERITANCE RULES
Virginia	Code of Virginia, §§64.1 et. seq.	All personal and real property in fee simple to surviving spouse unless decedent survived by children or their descendants who are not children of surviving spouse in which case 1/3 of personal and real property to surviving spouse and 2/3 to decedent's surviving children and their descendants.
Washington	Revised Code of Washington Annotated, §§11.02.005 et. seq.	100% of community property to surviving spouse; 1/2 of separate property to surviving spouse if surviving children; 3/4 of separate property to surviving spouse if surviving parents or siblings; 100% of separate property to surviving spouse if no surviving children, parents or siblings.
West Virginia	West Virginia Code, §§41-1-1 et. seq.	Dower interest of 1/3 of all real property as life estate to surviving spouse; 1/3 of all personal property to surviving spouse if surviving children or their descendants; 100% of all personal property and real property to surviving spouse if no surviving children or their descendants.
Wisconsin	Wisconsin Statutes Annotated, §§852.01 et. seq.	100% of estate to surviving spouse if no surviving children; first $25,000 plus 1/2 of balance of estate to surviving spouse if one surviving child of the marriage, or children of a deceased child of the marriage; first $25,000 plus 1/3 of balance of estate to surviving spouse if more than one surviving child of the marriage, or children of deceased child of the marriage; 1/2 of the estate to surviving spouse if surviving children not of the marriage, or children of a deceased child not of the marriage.

STATE	APPLICABLE STATUTE	BASIC INHERITANCE RULES
Wyoming	Wyoming Statutes Annotated, §§2-1-101 et. seq.	100% to surviving spouse if no surviving children or their descendants; 1/2 of estate to surviving spouse if surviving children and their descendants; 1/2 of estate to surviving spouse if surviving parents or siblings, but no surviving children or their descendants.

APPENDIX 3:
STATE LAW EXCEPTIONS TO
CONVENTIONAL PROBATE

STATE	APPLICABLE STATUTE	PROBATE EXEMPTION	SIMPLIFIED PROBATE
Alabama	Alabama Code, Title 43, Chapter 2, §§690, et. seq.	Not Available	Yes—up to $3,000 of personal property
Alaska	Alaska Statutes, Title 13, Chapter 6, §13.16.08	Not Available	Yes—no dollar limit
Arizona	Arizona Revised Statutes, §§14-3971, et. seq.	Yes—up to $30,000 of personal property	Not available except for certain types of family property
Arkansas	Arkansas Statutes Annotate, §§G2.2127et. seq.	Yes—up to $25,000	Not Available
California	California Probate Code, §§13200 et. seq.	Yes—up to $60,000 of personal property and real property interest $10,000	No dollar limit to surviving spouse on community property petition
Colorado	Colorado Revised Statutes, §§15-12-1201	Yes—up to $20,000 of net estate	Not available except for certain types of family property
Connecticut	Connecticut General Statutes Annotated, Title 45, §§266 et. seq.	Not Available	Yes—Up to $10,000 to spouse, next of kin, or creditor

STATE	APPLICABLE STATUTE	PROBATE EXEMPTION	SIMPLIFIED PROBATE
Delaware	Delaware Code Annotated, Title 12, §2306 et. seq.	Yes—up to $12,500 of personal property to spouse, grandparents, children or other statutory relative	Not Available
District of Columbia	District of Columbia Code, Title 20, §§2101 et. seq.	Not Available	Yes—up to $10,000 of personal property
Florida	Florida Statutes Annotated, §§735.103 et. seq.; 735.201 et. seq.; and 735.301 et. seq.	Not Available	Yes—Up to $25,000 of Florida property and up to $60,000 of estate to family members
Georgia	None	Not Available	Not Available
Hawaii	Hawaii Revised Statutes, §§560:3-1205 et. seq.; and 560:3-1213	Yes—up to $2,000	Yes—up to $20,000 of Hawaii property
Idaho	Idaho Code, §15-3-301 et. seq.	Not Available	Yes—no dollar limit
Illinois	Illinois Annotated Statutes, Chapter 110-1/2, §§6-8 et. seq.; 9-8 et. seq.; and 25-1 et. seq.	Yes—up to $25,000 of personal property; or if all beneficiaries are Illinois residents and are in agreement and no state of federal estate taxes are due	Yes—up to $50,000
Indiana	Indiana Statutes Annotated, §§27-1-7.5-5, et. seq.; and 29-1-8-2 et. seq.	Yes—up to $8,500 of personal property	Yes—no dollar limit

STATE	APPLICABLE STATUTE	PROBATE EXEMPTION	SIMPLIFIED PROBATE
Iowa	Iowa Code Annotated, §635 et. seq.	Not Available	Yes—up to $15,000 of total value of Iowa property to surviving spouse, minor children or parents only
Kansas	Kansas Statutes Annotated, §§59-3201 et. seq.; and 59-3301 et. seq.	Not Available	Yes—no dollar limit
Kentucky	Kentucky Revised Statutes, §§391.030 et. seq. and 395.450 et. seq.	Not Available	Yes—by agreement of all beneficiaries or when estate to spouse is under $7,500
Louisiana	No applicable statute	Not Available	Only if resident dies intestate with estate under $50,000
Maine	Maine Revised Statutes Annotated, Title 18A, §1-101	Not Available	Yes—no dollar limit
Maryland	Annotated Code of Maryland, §§5-601 et. seq.	Not available	Yes—up to $20,000
Massachusetts	Massachusetts General Laws Annotated, Chapter 195, §§16 et. seq.	Not Available	Yes—up to $15,000 of personal property
Michigan	Michigan Comp. Laws Annotated, §§9.1936; 27.5101, et. seq.; and 257.236	Not Available	Yes—up to $5,000
Minnesota	Minnesota Statutes Annotated, §§525.51 et. seq.	Not Available	Yes—up to $30,000
Mississippi	Mississippi Code Annotated, §91-7-147	Not Available	Yes—up to $500
Missouri	Missouri Statutes Annotated, §5-473.097	Not Available	Yes—up to $15,000

STATE	APPLICABLE STATUTE	PROBATE EXEMPTION	SIMPLIFIED PROBATE
Montana	Montana Code Annotated, Title 72, §§3-201 et. seq.	Not Available	Yes—up to $15,000
Nebraska	Revised Statutes of Nebraska, §§30-2414 et. seq.	Not Available	Yes—no dollar limit
Nevada	Nevada Revised Statutes, §§145.070 et. seq. and 146.010 et. seq.	Yes—up to $25,000	Yes—up to $100,000
New Hampshire	New Hampshire Revised Statutes Annotated, Chapter 553,331 et. seq.	Not Available except up to $500 to surviving spouse	Yes—up to $5,000
New Jersey	No applicable statute	Not available except $10,000 to spouse and $5,000 to others if resident dies intestate	Not Available
New Mexico	New Mexico Statutes, §§45-3-1202 and 45-3-1204	Yes—up to $5,000	Yes—up to $10,000
New York	Consolidated Laws of New York Annotated, EPTL §§1301 et. seq.	Yes—up to $10,000 and certain exempt property	Not Available
North Carolina	General Statutes of North Carolina, Chapter 28A, §25-1.1	Yes—up to $10,000 personal property	Not Available
North Dakota	North Dakota Code, §§30.1-14 et. seq.	Not Available	Yes—no dollar limit
Ohio	Ohio Revised Code Annotated, §2113.02	Not Available	Yes—up to $15,000
Oklahoma	Oklahoma Statutes Annotated, Title 58, §§241 et. seq.	Not Available	Yes—up to $60,000

STATE	APPLICABLE STATUTE	PROBATE EXEMPTION	SIMPLIFIED PROBATE
Oregon	Oregon Revised Statutes, §§114.515 et. seq.	Yes—up to $15,000 personal property and $35,000 real property	Not Available
Pennsylvania	Pennsylvania Statutes Annotated, Title 20, §§3102 et. seq.	Not Available	Yes—up to $10,000 personal property
Rhode Island	No applicable statute	Not Available	Not Available
South Carolina	Code of Laws of South Carolina, Title 62, Chapter 3, §§1201 and 1203 et. seq.	Yes—up to $10,000	Yes—up to $10,000
South Dakota	South Dakota Codified Laws, §§30-11A et. seq.; and 30-11-1	Yes—up to $5,000	Yes—up to $60,000
Tennessee	Tennessee Code Annotated, Title 30, Chapter 4, §§101 et. seq.	Not Available	Yes—up to $10,000 real property
Texas	Texas Probate Code, §§137 et. seq. and 145 et. seq.	Yes—up to $50,000	Yes—no dollar limit
Utah	Utah Code, Title 75, §3-301	Not Available	Yes—no dollar limit
Vermont	Vermont Statutes Annotated, Title 14, §§1901 et. seq.	Not Available	Yes—up to $10,000 personal property
Virginia	Code of Virginia, §§64.1-132 et. seq.	Yes—up to $5,000 personal property and $5,000 wages or bank account	Not Available

STATE	APPLICABLE STATUTE	PROBATE EXEMPTION	SIMPLIFIED PROBATE
Washington	Revised Code of Washington Annotated, Title 11, §§62.010 et. seq.	Yes—up to $10,000 personal property	Not Available
West Virginia	West Virginia Code, Chapter 24, Article 2, §1	Not Available	Yes—up to $50,000
Wisconsin	Wisconsin Statutes Annotated, §§867.03 et. seq. and 867.045 et. seq.	Yes—up to $5,000 personal property	Yes—up to $10,000
Wyoming	Wyoming Statutes Annotated, §2-1-201	Yes—up to $30,000	Not Available

APPENDIX 4:
SAMPLE FIDUCIARY BOND

OSM CODE: BND

STATE OF MICHIGAN PROBATE COURT COUNTY CIRCUIT COURT - FAMILY DIVISION	BOND OF FIDUCIARY	FILE NO.

Estate of _____

1. The principal has been appointed _____ , accepts the duties of this appointment and,
   Type of fiduciary
   with the surety(ies), agrees to pay $ _____ to the State of Michigan as obligee for the benefit of the
   persons interested in the estate if the principal fails to discharge all duties according to law.

2. The surety(ies) agree to be jointly and severally liable on the bond with the principal and with each other.

3. The surety(ies) consent to the jurisdiction of the court that issued letters of authority to the principal in a proceeding pertaining to the principal's fiduciary duties.

4. If this is a bond for a special personal representative who is subsequently appointed personal representative, the obligations and liabilities of this bond remain in effect.

Date _____

Principal signature _____

Attorney name (type or print)	Bar no.	Principal name (type or print)	
Address		Address	
City, state, zip	Telephone no.	City, state, zip	Telephone no.

Surety signature _____   Surety signature _____

Surety name (type or print)		Surety name (type or print)	
Address		Address	
City, state, zip	Telephone no.	City, state, zip	Telephone no.

Oath of Personal Surety The surety acknowledges personal worth of the amount of the penalty in the bond over and above all debts and legal exemptions.

Subscribed and sworn to before me on _____ , _____ County, Michigan.
Date

My commission expires: _____   Signature: _____
Date   Notary public/Deputy probate register

_____

Do not write below this line - For court use only

I have examined and approve this bond.

Date _____

Judge/Probate register _____   Bar no. _____

☐ No new letters of authority are to be issued.

PC 570 (3/00) **BOND OF FIDUCIARY**

MCL 700.3601; MSA 27.13601; MCL 700.3604; MSA 27.13604; MCL 700.5106(3); MSA 27.15106(3); MCL 700.5410; MSA 27.15410, MCL 700.5411; MSA 27.15411

APPENDIX 5:
SAMPLE PETITION FOR LETTERS
FOR ADMINISTRATION

SURROGATE'S COURT OF THE STATE OF NEW YORK
COUNTY OF
--X
ADMINISTRATION PROCEEDING,   PETITION FOR LETTERS OF:

Estate of   [ ]   Administration
                                                    [ ]   Limited Administration
a/k/a   [ ]   Administration with Limitations
                                                    [ ]   Temporary Administration
                                    Deceased.   File No.
--X

TO THE SURROGATE'S COURT, COUNTY OF

It is respectfully alleged:

1. The name, domicile and interest in this proceeding of the petitioner, who is of full age, is as follows:

Name: _____

Domicile: _____
                        (Street Number)   (City, Village/Town)

_____
                (State)   (Zip Code)

Citizenship (check one):   [   ] U.S.A.   [   ] Other (specify)

Interest of Petitioner (check one):

    [   ] Distributee of decedent (state relationship)

    [   ] Other (specify)

Is proposed Administrator an attorney?   [   ] Yes   [   ] No
[If yes, submit statement pursuant to 22 NYCRR 207.16(e); see also 207.52 (Accounting of attorney-fiduciary).]

2. The name, domicile, date and place of death, and national citizenship of the above-named decedent are as follows: [**The Death Certificate must be filed with this proceeding.** If the decedent's domicile is different from that shown on the death certificate, check box [   ] and attach an affidavit explaining the reason for this inconsistency.]

Name: _____

Domicile: _____
                        (Street Number)   (City, Village/Town)

_____
                (State)   (Zip Code)

Township of: _____ County of: _____

Date of Death: _____ Place of Death: _____

Citizenship: (check one): [   ] U.S.A.   [   ] Other (specify)

-1-

[Note: For Items 3a through c: Do not include any assets that are jointly held, held in trust for another, or have a named beneficiary.]

3.(a)   The estimated gross value of the decedent's personal property passing by intestacy is less than

$

(b)   The estimated gross value of the decedent's real property, in this state, which is [   ] improved,
[   ] unimproved, passing by intestacy is less than

$

A brief description of each parcel is as follows:

(c)   The estimated gross rent for a period of eighteen (18) months is the sum of

$

(d)   In addition to the value of the personal property stated in paragraph (3) the following right of action existed on behalf of the decedent and survived his/her death, or is granted to the administrator of the decedent by special provision of law, and it is impractical to give a bond sufficient to cover the probable amount to be recovered therein: [Write "NONE or state briefly the cause of action and the person against whom it exists, including names and carrier].

(e) death,   If decedent is survived by a spouse and a parent, or parents but no issue, and there is a claim for wrongful check here [   ] and furnish names(s) and address(es) of parent(s) in Paragraph 7. See EPTL 5-4.4.

4.   A diligent search and inquiry, including a search of any safe deposit box, has been made for a will of the decedent and none has been found. Petitioner(s) (has) (have) been unable to obtain any information concerning any will of the decedent and therefore allege(s), upon information and belief, that the decedent died without leaving any last will.

5.   A search of the records of this Court shows that no application has ever been made for letters of administration upon the estate of the decedent or for the probate of a will of the decedent, and your petitioner is informed and verily believes that no such application ever has been made to the Surrogate's Court of any other county of this state.

6.   The decedent left surviving the following who would inherit his/her estate pursuant to EPTL 4-1.1 and 4-1.2:

    a.   [   ] Spouse (husband/wife).

    b.   [   ] Child or children or descendants of predeceased child or children. [Must include marital, nonmarital and adopted].

       c.   [   ] Any issue of the decedent adopted by persons related to the decedent (DRL Section 117).

       d.   [   ] Mother/Father.

       e.   [   ] Sisters or brothers, either of whole or half blood, and issue of predeceased sisters or brothers.

       f.   [   ] Grandmother/Grandfather.

       g.   [   ] Aunts or uncles, and children of predeceased aunts and uncles (first cousins).

       h.   [   ] First cousins once removed (children of first cousins).

[Information is required only as to those classes of surviving relatives who would take the property of decedent pursuant to EPTL 4-1.1. State "number" of survivors in each class. Insert "No" in all prior classes. Insert "X" in all subsequent classes].

-2-

7.   The decedent left surviving the following distributees, or other necessary parties, whose names, degrees of relationship, domiciles, post office address and citizenship are as follows:

[Note: Show clearly how each person is related to decedent. If relationship is through an ancestor who is deceased, give name, date of death, and relationship of the ancestor to the decedent. Use rider sheet if space in paragraph (7) is not sufficient. See Uniform Rules 207.16(b).

If any person listed in paragraph (7) is a nonmarital person, or descended from a nonmarital person, attach a copy of the order of filiation or Schedule A. If any person listed in paragraph (7) was adopted by any persons related by blood or marriage to decedent or descended from such persons, attach Schedule B].

7a.   The following are of full age and under no disability: [If nonmarital or adopted-out person, so indicate by attaching Schedule A and/or B]

Name	Relationship	Domicile and Citizenship	Mailing Address

7b.   The following are infants and/or persons under disability: [Attach applicable Schedule A, B, C, and/or D]

Name	Relationship	Domicile and Citizenship	Mailing Address

8.   There are no outstanding debts or funeral expenses, except: [Write "NONE" or state same]

9. There are no other persons interested in this proceeding other than those hereinbefore mentioned.

WHEREFORE, your petitioner respectfully prays that: [Check and complete all relief requested]

( ) a.   process issue to all necessary parties to show cause why letters should not be issued as requested;

( ) b.   an order be granted dispensing with service of process upon those persons named in Paragraph (7) who have a right to letters prior or equal to that of the person nominated, and who are non-domiciliaries or whose names or whereabouts are unknown and cannot be ascertained;

( ) c.   a decree award Letters of:

   [ ] Administration to

   [ ] Limited Administration to

   [ ] Administration with Limitation to

   [ ] Temporary Administration to

or to such other person or persons having a prior right as may be entitled thereto, and;

( ) d. That the authority of the representative under the forgoing Letters be limited with respect to the prosecution or enforcement of a cause of action on behalf of the estate, as follows: the administrator(s) may not enforce a judgement or receive any funds without further order of the Surrogate.

( ) e. That the authority of the representative under the foregoing Letters be limited as follows:

( ) f. [State any other relief requested.]

Dated:

1.   2.

   (Signature of Petitioner)   (Signature of Petitioner)

   (Print Name)   (Print Name)

STATE OF NEW YORK	)	
	)	ss:
COUNTY OF	)	

COMBINED VERIFICATION, OATH AND DESIGNATION
[For use when petitioner is to be appointed administrator]

I, the undersigned the petitioner named in the foregoing petition, being duly sworn, say:

1. VERIFICATION: I have read the foregoing petition subscribed by me and know the contents thereof, and the same is true of my own knowledge, except as to the matters therein stated to be alleged upon information and belief, and as to those matters I believe it to be true.

2. OATH OF ADMINISTRATOR as indicated above: I am over eighteen (18) years of age and a citizen of the United States; and I will well, faithfully and honestly discharge the duties of Administrator of the goods, chattels and credits of said decedent according to law. I am not ineligible to receive letters and will duly account for all moneys and other property that will come into my hands.

3. DESIGNATION OF CLERK FOR SERVICE OF PROCESS: I do hereby designate the Clerk of the Surrogate's Court of _____ County, and his/her successor in office, as a person on whom service of any process, issuing from such Surrogate's Court may be made in like manner and with like effect as if it were served personally upon me, whenever I cannot be found and served within the State of New York after due diligence used.

My domicile is:

(Street/Number)	(City, Village/Town)	(State)	(Zip)

_____
Signature of Petitioner

On the _____ day of _____ , 20 ___ , before me personally came

to me known to be the person described in and who executed the foregoing instrument. Such person duly swore to such instrument before me and duly acknowledged that he/she executed the same.

Notary Public
Commission Expires:
(Affix Notary Stamp or Seal)

Signature of Attorney:

Print Name:

Firm Name: _____   Tel. No.:

Address of Attorney:

File #

SURROGATE'S COURT OF THE STATE OF NEW YORK
COUNTY OF
---X
PROCEEDING FOR
Estate of

a/k/a

Deceased.
---X

SCHEDULE A
NONMARITAL PERSONS
(PERSONS BORN OUT OF WEDLOCK)

[NOTE: Nonmarital children (or their issue) who would be distributees if they (or their ancestors) were born in wedlock will not be regarded as distributees unless satisfactory proof is submitted establishing paternity]. See EPTL 4-1.2 which sets forth methods of establishing paternity.

Name of alleged distributee:

Date of birth: Relationship to decedent:

Name of father:

Name of mother:

Does the birth certificate contain the father's name?   Yes [   ]   No [   ]

   If yes, attach copy of birth certificate.

Has an order of filiation establishing paternity been entered?
Yes [   ]   No [   ]   If yes, attach copy of order.

Did the nonmarital person live with his or her father?   Yes [   ]   No [   ]

   If yes, give dates and places of residence:

File #

SURROGATE'S COURT OF THE STATE OF NEW YORK
COUNTY OF
---X

PROCEEDING FOR   SCHEDULE B
Estate of   ISSUE OF THE DECEDENT
                                                               WHO WERE THE SUBJECT
a/k/a   OF AN ADOPTION

                              Deceased.
---X

Name of Child:

Relationship to Decedent Prior to Adoption:

Date of adoption:

Was this a step-parent adoption? (i.e., was the child adopted by the spouse of the decedent's former spouse?)
Yes [   ]   No [   ]

If yes, name of adoptive father or mother:

If not a step-parent adoption, indicate below the biological relationship of the adoptive parent to the child:

[   ] grandparent(s)

[   ] brother or sister

[   ] aunt or uncle

[   ] first cousin

[   ] nephew or niece

Name of the adoptive parent:

File #

SURROGATE'S COURT OF THE STATE OF NEW YORK
COUNTY OF
---X
PROCEEDING FOR   SCHEDULE C
Estate of   INFANTS

a/k/a

Deceased.
---X

[NOTE: Please furnish all of the information requested, otherwise the petition may be rejected.]

Name: _____

Date of birth:

Relationship to
the decedent:

With whom does the
infant reside?

Name of mother: _____   Is she alive?

Name of Father: _____   Is he alive?

Does infant have a court-appointed guardian?   Yes [   ]   No [   ]

Name and address of guardian:_____

Date of birth:

Relationship to
the decedent:

File #

SURROGATE'S COURT OF THE STATE OF NEW YORK
COUNTY OF
---X
PROCEEDING FOR   SCHEDULE D
Estate of   PERSONS UNDER DISABILITY
                                                                OTHER THAN INFANTS

a/k/a

Deceased.
---X

[use additional sheets if more than one]

1. Name: Relationship:

    Residence:

    With whom does this person reside?

    If this person is in prison, name of prison:

    Does this person have a court-appointed fiduciary?   Yes [   ]   No [   ]

    If yes, give name, title and address:

    If no, describe nature of disability:

    If no, give name and address of relative or friend interested in his or her welfare:

2. Whereabouts unknown/Unknowns [persons whose addresses or names are unknown to petitioner; if known, give name   and relationship to decedent]

APPENDIX 6:
SAMPLE NOTICES TO CREDITORS

CC23

District Court
CLARK COUNTY, NEVADA

In the Matter of the Estate of

Deceased.

CASE NO. _____

NOTICE TO CREDITORS
(____ Day Notice)

Notice is hereby given that on the __ ___ day of _____, _____, the undersigned was duly appointed and qualified by the above-entitled Court as Personal Representative of the Estate of _____ _____, Deceased. All creditors having claims against the Estate are required to file their claims, with supporting documentation attached, with the Clerk of the Court, Clark County Courthouse, 200 South Third Street, Las Vegas. Nevada 89155, within _____ days after the mailing or the first publication (as the case may be) of this Notice.

DATED this _____ day of _____, _____.

_____
Signature of Personal Representative

_____

_____

(Type Name & Address)

Submitted By:

_____
(SIGNATURE)

Name _____
Address: _____
City/State/Zip: _____
Telephone: _____
Attorney for the Estate

REV 6/01/cc

APPENDIX 7:
SAMPLE AFFIDAVIT OF PUBLICATION

AFFP

District Court
Clark County, Nevada

AFFIDAVIT OF PUBLICATION

State of_____)
) ss:
County of _____)

_____, being first duly sworn, deposes and says:

     That she/he is a legal clerk for_____, daily newspaper(s)

regularly issued, published and circulated in the city(ies) of_____.

and that the advertisement, a true copy of which is attached, was continuously published in the _____

for a period of _____ insertions from the period of _____ to _____ on the

following days:

_____

_____

_____

_____

Signed:_____

Subscribed and sworn to before me this

_____ day of_____, _____

_____
Notary Public

Rev 6/01/cc

APPENDIX 8:
SAMPLE ORDER APPROVING THE PETITION AND ISSUING LETTERS OF ADMINISTRATION

PRESENT:
HON. _____ Surrogate.
_____X
ADMINISTRATION PROCEEDING
Estate of

a/k/a
_____ Deceased.
_____X

DECREE APPOINTING
ADMINISTRATOR

File No. _____

A petition having been filed by _____ praying that administration of the goods, chattels

and credits of the above-named decedent be granted to _____; and all persons named in such

petition, required to be cited, having been duly cited to show cause why such relief should not be granted or having duly waived

the issuance of such citation and consented thereto; and it appearing that _____

is in all respects competent to act as administrator of the estate of said deceased, and a

[ ] bond having been filed and approved in the amount of $
[ ] bond having been dispensed with

and such representative(s) otherwise having qualified therefore; now, after due deliberation, with no one appearing in

opposition thereto, it is

ORDERED AND DECREED that Letters of Administration issue to

ORDERED AND DECREED, that the authority of such representative(s) be restricted in accordance with, and that letters herein issued contain, the limitation, if any, which appears immediately below.

_____
HON. _____ Surrogate

APPENDIX 9:
ESTATE PLANNING GUIDE

BACKGROUND INFORMATION

Name:

Address:

Telephone:

IMMEDIATE FAMILY

Spouse Name:

Address (if different from above):

Telephone (if different from above):

Child #1—Name:

Address (if different from above):

Telephone (if different from above):

Child #2—Name:

Address (if different from above):

Telephone (if different from above):

Child #3—Name:

Address (if different from above):

Telephone (if different from above):

Child #4—Name:

Address (if different from above):

Telephone (if different from above):

Last Employer—Husband

Name:

Address:

Telephone:

Last Employer—Wife

Name:

Address:

Telephone:

Attorney

Name:

Address:

Telephone:

Accountant

Name:

Address:

Telephone:

Additional Important Contacts

Name:

Address:

Telephone:

Relationship:

Name:

Address:

Telephone:

Relationship:

Name:

Address:

Telephone:

Relationship:

INCOME/PENSIONS/INVESTMENTS

Social Security

Local Office Address:

Telephone:

Husband's Social Security Number:

Wife's Social Security Number:

Child #1—Social Security Number:

Child #2—Social Security Number:

Child #3—Social Security Number:

Child #4—Social Security Number:

Estimated Monthly Survivor's Benefit:

Estimated Death Benefit:

Pensions

Employer Name:

Address:

Telephone:

Details:

Employer Name:

Address:

Telephone:

Details:

Annuity Plans

Company Name:

Address:

Telephone:

Company Representative:

Company Name:

Address:

Telephone:

Company Representative:

Veteran's Benefits

Local VA Office Address:

Telephone:

Identification Number:

Savings Accounts

Bank Name:

Address:

Telephone:

Bank Representative:

Account Number:

Name(s) On Account:

Location of Passbook and/or Statements:

Bank Name:

Address:

Telephone:

Bank Representative:

Account Number:

Name(s) On Account:

Location of Passbook and/or Statements:

Checking Accounts

Bank Name:

Address:

Telephone:

Bank Representative:

Account Number:

Name(s) On Account:

Location of Checkbook and/or Statements:

Bank Name:

Address:

Telephone:

Bank Representative:

Account Number:

Name(s) On Account:

Location of Checkbook and/or Statements:

Savings Certificates

Bank Name:

Address:

Telephone:

Bank Representative:

Certificate Number:

Name(s) On Certificate:

Due Date:

Value:

Location of Certificate:

Bank Name:

Address:

Telephone:

Bank Representative:

Certificate Number:

Name(s) On Certificate:

Due Date:

Value:

Location of Certificate:

Credit Union Accounts

Credit Union Name:

Address:

Telephone:

Contact:

Account Number:

Name(s) On Account:

Location of Passbook or Statements:

Credit Union Name:

Address:

Telephone:

Contact:

Account Number:

Name(s) On Account:

Location of Passbook or Statements:

Stocks

Brokerage Firm Name:

Address:

Telephone:

Broker Name:

Name of Stock:

Number of Shares:

Brokerage Firm Name:

Address:

Telephone:

Broker Name:

Name of Stock:

Number of Shares:

Bonds

Brokerage Firm Name:

Address:

Telephone:

Broker Name:

Description of Bond:

Serial Number:

Face Value:

Brokerage Firm Name:

Address:

Telephone:

Broker Name:

Description of Bond:

Serial Number:

Face Value:

Individual Retirement Accounts

Company Name:

Address:

Telephone:

Account No:

Account Name:

Company Name:

Address:

Telephone:

Account No:

Account Name:

Safety Deposit Box

Bank Name:

Address:

Telephone:

Bank Representative:

Key Number:

Location of Key:

Person(s) Authorized to Open Box:

Contents of Box:

INSURANCE COVERAGE

Life Insurance—Husband

Employer Plan

Amount:

Beneficiary:

Additional Life Insurance

Company Name:

Address:

Telephone:

Insurance Agent:

Policy No:

Premium Amount and Due Date:

Value of Policy:

Beneficiary:

Location of Policy:

Life Insurance—Wife

Employer Plan

Amount:

Beneficiary:

Additional Life Insurance

Company Name:

Address:

Telephone:

Insurance Agent:

Policy No:

Premium Amount and Due Date:

Value of Policy:

Beneficiary:

Location of Policy:

Health and Disability Insurance

Company Name:

Address:

Telephone:

Policy No:

Policyholder:

Premium Amount and Due Date:

Homeowners Policy

Company Name:

Address:

Telephone:

Agent:

Policy No:

Premium Amount and Due Date:

Value of Policy:

Location of Policy:

Automobile Insurance

Car #1

Make/Model/Year of Car

Vehicle Identification Number:

Title Owner:

Registration Name:

Listed Drivers:

Company Name:

Address:

Telephone:

Agent:

Policy No:

Premium Amount and Due Date:

Value of Policy:

Location of Policy:

Car #2

Make/Model/Year of Car

Vehicle Identification Number:

Title Owner:

Registration Name:

Listed Drivers:

Company Name:

Address:

Telephone:

Agent:

Policy No:

Premium Amount and Due Date:

Value of Policy:

Location of Policy:

REAL PROPERTY

Your Home

Lender Name:

Address:

Telephone:

Contact:

Account No:

Monthly Payment and Due Date:

Location of Ownership Documents:

Other Real Property

Lender Name:

Address:

Telephone:

Contact:

Account No:

Monthly Payment and Due Date:

Location of Ownership Documents:

Cemetery Plot

Site and Description:

Lot No:

Ownership Documents:

Site and Description:

Lot No:

Ownership Documents:

Automobile Titles

Car #1

Make/Model/Year of Car

Vehicle Identification Number:

Lender:

Address:

Telephone:

Monthly Payment and Due Date:

Title Owner:

Location of Title Documents:

Car #2

Make/Model/Year of Car

Vehicle Identification Number:

Lender:

Address:

Telephone:

Monthly Payment and Due Date:

Title Owner:

Location of Title Documents:

CREDIT

Credit Cards

Name of Creditor:

Address:

Telephone Number:

Credit Holder:

Account No:

Name of Creditor:

Address:

Telephone Number:

Credit Holder:

Account No:

Name of Creditor:

Address:

Telephone Number:

Credit Holder:

Account No:

Name of Creditor:

Address:

Telephone Number:

Credit Holder:

Account No:

Personal Debts

Entity/Individual Owed

Name:

Address:

Telephone:

Account No:

Amount:

Due Date:

Details:

Entity/Individual Owed

Name:

Address:

Telephone:

Account No:

Amount:

Due Date:

Details:

FUNERAL/MEMORIAL ARRANGEMENTS

Husband

Funeral Home

Name:

Address:

Telephone:

Contact:

Cemetery Location:

Lot No:

Services

Memorial Location:

Funeral Location:

Religious Services Location:

Additional Comments:

Cremation (If applicable)

Contact:

Telephone:

Additional Comments:

Body Donation (If applicable)

Contact:

Telephone:

Location of Signed Donor Cards:

Additional Comments:

Organ Donation (If applicable)

Contact:

Telephone:

Location of Signed Donor Cards:

Additional Comments:

Wife

Funeral Home

Name:

Address:

Telephone:

Contact:

Cemetery Location:

Lot No:

Services

Memorial Location:

Funeral Location:

Religious Services Location:

Additional Comments:

Cremation (If applicable)

Contact:

Telephone:

Additional Comments:

Body Donation (If applicable)

Contact:

Telephone:

Location of Signed Donor Cards:

Additional Comments:

Organ Donation (If applicable)

Contact:

Telephone:

Location of Signed Donor Cards:

Additional Comments:

WILLS

Husband

Preparer Name:

Address:

Telephone:

Date Prepared:

Executor Name:

Address:

Telephone:

Location of Original Will:

Location of Copies:

Wife

Preparer Name:

Address:

Telephone:

Date Prepared:

Executor Name:

Address:

Telephone:

Location of Original Will:

Location of Copies:

PERSONAL EFFECTS

Location of Other Important Documents

Birth Certificate(s)

Marriage/Divorce Certificate(s):

Citizenship Papers:

Military Papers:

Tax Records:

Bank Books:

Location of Valuables/Personal Property

Item #1 Description:

Location:

Item #2 Description:

Location:

Item #3 Description:

Location:

Item #4 Description:

Location:

Item #5 Description:

Location:

Note: Attach Additional Sheets if Necessary

NOTES AND SPECIAL INSTRUCTIONS

APPENDIX 10:
SAMPLE INVENTORY AND APPRAISAL

CC25

District Court
CLARK COUNTY, NEVADA

In the Matter of the Estate of

}

CASE NO. _____

Deceased

INVENTORY, APPRAISAL AND RECORD OF VALUE

	(1) Gross Asset Value	(2) Amount of Encumbrance	Estate's* Interest	(1 Less 2) Net VALUE of Estate's Interest
A. REAL PROPERTY - Description				
1 _____	$	$	% ( )	$
2 _____				
3. _____				
B. PERSONAL PROPERTY Cash and deposits (list)				
4 _____				
5 _____				
6 _____				
Partnership interests, etc. (describe)				
7 _____				
8 _____				
Notes, bonds, securities, debts, etc. (list name & address of debtor, date debt originated, endorsement w/date, estimate as to amount collectible)				
9. _____				
10. _____				
11. _____				
12 _____				
Vehicles (describe)				
13. _____				
14 _____				
15 _____				
Misc. Personal Property (describe)				
16. _____				
17 _____				

Designate nature of estate's interest & % of ownership (C) community; (S) separate; i.e. 50% (C) or (S).

STATE OF NEVADA)
COUNTY OF CLARK) ss:

OATH OF APPRAISER

I, the undersigned, appraiser of the Estate of the above-named Decedent, solemnly affirm that I will truly, honestly, and impartially appraise the inventory of the estate to the best of my knowledge and ability.

SUBSCRIBED AND AFFIRMED to before me this

_____ day of _____._____

_____
NOTARY PUBLIC

_____
Appraiser

_____
(Type name & address)

APPRAISAL

I, the undersigned appraiser of the Estate of the above-named Decedent, hereby certify that items _____ of the inventory of the estate have been examined by me and that I appraised these items on the inventory at the value shown opposite thereof for a total sum of _____ ($_____) Dollars.

_____   _____
Appraiser   **Date**

(Repeat Oath & Certification for each Appraiser, attach separate sheets if necessary)

STATE OF NEVADA)
COUNTY OF CLARK) ss:

OATH OF PERSONAL REPRESENTATIVE

I, the undersigned Personal Representative of the Estate of the above-named Decedent, solemnly affirm that the foregoing inventory is a true statement of all assets of the Estate which have come into my possession or of which I have knowledge and includes all money and claims of the Deceased.

SUBSCRIBED AND AFFIRMED to before me this

_____ day of _____._____

_____
Personal Representative

_____
NOTARY PUBLIC

VERIFIED RECORD OF VALUE IN LIEU OF APPRAISEMENT

I, the undersigned, solemnly affirm that items _____ of the inventory of the Estate have been examined by me and that I recorded the value of these items on the inventory at the value shown opposite thereof for a total sum of_____
_____ ($_____) dollars.

_____
Personal Representative

STATE OF NEVADA)
COUNTY OF CLARK) ss:

The undersigned being duly sworn states that he is the Personal Representative of the Estate of the above-named ward; that he has read the above and foregoing Record of Value, knows the contents thereof, and that the same is true of his/her own knowledge, except for those matters therein stated on information and belief, and as for those matters he believes them to be true.

SUBSCRIBED AND AFFIRMED to before me this

_____ day of _____._____

_____
Personal Representative

_____
NOTARY PUBLIC

REV 6/01/cc

APPENDIX 11:
SAMPLE CLAIM FOR STATE TAX REFUND

SURROGATE'S COURT OF THE STATE OF NEW YORK
COUNTY OF
---x
In the Matter of the Application of
_____, as Administrat(or)(rix),   PETITION
of the Goods, Chattels and Credits which   File No.
were of_____   (As of 4/98)
                  deceased,

For leave to compromise a certain cause
of action for wrongful death of the decedent
and to render and have judicially settled
an account of the proceedings as such
Administrator
---x

TO THE SURROGATE'S COURT:

It is respectfully alleged:

1.   Petitioner_____is the_____of the above-named
      decedent and presently resides at_____
      _____.

2.   The decedent died a resident of _____, County of _____, New
      York on _____; and had resided there with _____
      _____

3.   On_____, Letters of Guardianship of the person and property of
      _____, infant son/daughter of the decedent (copy attached),
      were issued to your petitioner by the Surrogate's Court, _____County.

4.   On _____, Limited Letters of Administration of the Goods, Chattels and
      Credits which were of _____, deceased, were issued to petitioner by the
      Surrogate's Court of _____County, which letters were of limited
      authority and restrained your petitioner from compromising or collecting upon
      said claim for wrongful death until further order of this court. To date, said letters
      have not been revoked and are presently in full force and effect. No bond was
      required of your administrator to cover any probable amount to be realized from
      said action.

5.   The decedent at the time of death was employed as a _____by
      at _____, earning approximately $_____ per week.

6.   The decedent at the time of death was _____years of age, having been
      born on _____.

7.   The injuries that resulted in the decedent's death were sustained on [give date,
      time] _____ at [location] _____.

      [Describe fatal incident]

8.   The decedent was taken to _____ Hospital where he/she died
      on _____ at or about _____ a.m./p.m. of that day without having
      regained consciousness. [Describe circumstances, e.g., length of hospitalization,
      etc., resulting in death] Decedent did not regain consciousness, and all of the
      proceeds of the settlement of the action are to be allocated for wrongful death
      and not for conscious pain and suffering.

WD-2 (4/98)   - 1 -

9. A combined action for decedent's wrongful death and conscious pain and suffering was commenced against the defendant _____.
[Include references to court where action commenced, pleadings, etc.] Thereafter, negotiations were entered into with the representative of _____ Insurance Company, and a final offer has been made to settle this claim for the sum of $ _____ out of maximum insurance coverage of $ _____.

10. An investigation of the personal resources of the defendant, _____, has been undertaken and it has been discovered that [provide details as to assets]_____.

11. Petitioner believes that it is in the best interests of the distributees and the estate of the decedent and those interested therein to accept the settlement so offered and that this is the largest amount that can be obtained without further litigation.

12. The grounds of petitioner's belief are [indicate reasons why acceptance of the settlement is advisable]

13. The decedent at the time of death was married and left the following survivors:

Name	Relationship	Date of Birth	Present Age

14. On _____, petitioner retained _____, Esq. of _____, as his/her attorney (a copy of the retainer agreement and affidavit of legal services are attached). In view of the results achieved, petitioner would request the court to approve a fee as follows: That the attorney's disbursements in the sum of $ _____ first be deducted from the gross settlement of _____ ; that of the balance of $ _____ a fee of _____ % or $ _____ be allowed, which together with disbursements of $ _____ would amount to total compensation of $ _____.

15. Petitioner has been advised that the proceeds of an action for wrongful death are allocated according to the pecuniary loss sustained by the widow/widower and infants. Petitioner has further been advised that the share of the petitioner and the children are computed in accordance with the years of dependency each of the survivors could look forward to but for the decedent's death. At the time of death, decedent was _____ years of age, having been born on _____ and having died on _____ and had a life expectancy of _____ years, based on the table of vital statistics, United States Health Department - copy attached. As petitioner as husband/wife and widower/widow was born on _____ and had a life expectancy of years, the life expectancy of the decedent must be used. Therefore, the years of dependency are as follows:

Name	Age on Date of Death	Anticipated Years of Dependency	Percentage of Net Amount of Settlement

NOTE: WHERE RECOVERY OR PART THEREOF IS ALLOCATED TO CONSCIOUS PAIN AND SUFFERING, THE PROCEEDS PASS THROUGH THE DECEDENT'S ESTATE EITHER IN ACCORDANCE WITH THE PROVISIONS OF HIS/HER WILL, OR IN THE EVENT OF INTESTACY, IN ACCORDANCE WITH EPTL 4-1.1.

WD-2 (4/98)   - 2 -

16.   All of the above persons are of sound mind and full age (except for the infant _____) and are citizens of the United States.

17.   Petitioner as administrat(or)(rix) hereby waives any claim for statutory commissions and waives the filing of a surety bond.

18.   Decedent's funeral bill in the sum of $ _____ has been paid by_____. Annexed hereto is the paid bill. No reimbursement is sought. There are no medical bills or hospital bills outstanding, and there are no assignments, compensation claims or liens filed with petitioner as administrator except for the following:

    a)   The Commissioner of Social Services has submitted a claim of $ _____ for public assistance rendered to decedent and his/her family for the years _____. This claim is rejected since the Department would have a lien only against a recovery for conscious pain and suffering, which would be an estate asset, and here there is to be no recovery for conscious pain and suffering.

    b)   _____has submitted a claim for _____based on an _____. This claim is also rejected for the same reasons as the rejection of the claim of the Department of Social Services.

    [List other creditors, if any]

    c)   Decedent's father/mother, _____, seeks a share of the recovery by claiming the suffering of a pecuniary loss by virtue of decedent's death. This claim is rejected on the grounds that in spite of any possible demonstrated pecuniary injury, decedent's father/mother is nevertheless a nondistributee and thus ineligible to share in the recovery.

19.   [If applicable] During the years through _____, the decedent was the recipient of public assistance in the form of Aid to Dependent Children.

20.   No previous application has been made for the relief sought herein.

21.   Petitioner desires leave of this court to compromise and settle with _____ Insurance Company the claim against _____ for the wrongful death of the decedent, to discontinue the action for conscious pain and suffering and to fix reasonable attorney's fees and to pay the distributees their share of the settlement pursuant to the provisions of law (and to settle the account of the Administrat(or)(rix).

22.   The only persons interested in this proceeding entitled to notice thereof are the following:

Name	Address	Relationship
		Husband
		Administrator
		Wife
		Administratrix
		Daughter
		Son

Name	Address	Relationship
		Father
		Mother
		Alleged Creditor
	New York City Department of Social Services	Possible Creditor
	New York State Tax Commission	Possible Creditor Defendant
	Insurance Company	Defendant's Insurance Company

None of the above are under a disability except _____, an infant under the age of fourteen years.

23. Petitioner has not become interested in the within matter at the instance of the defendant or anyone acting on defendant's behalf, directly or indirectly.

WHEREFORE your petitioner prays that a Citation herein be directed to the following:

Name   _____ Address

[List names of distributees and, if applicable, New York City Department of Social Services, New York State Tax Commission, Defendant, and Defendant's Insurance Company.]

requiring them to show cause as follows: [include as applicable]

WHY the administrator should not be authorized and empowered to compromise and settle a certain claim for the wrongful death of the decedent, against _____ _____for the sum of $ _____ to discontinue the action for conscious pain and suffering, and

WHY the entire recovery of $ _____ should not be allocated to the cause of action for decedent's wrongful death, and

WHY the provisions in the Letters of Administration heretofore issued to your petitioner on _____restraining the administrator from compromising or collecting upon the aforesaid claim should not be modified to permit said compromise, and

WHY the filing of a bond should not be dispensed with, and

WHY the account of   , as Administrator in this proceeding, should not be judicially settled, and

WHY defendant, _____, or defendant's insurance company should not pay to the firm of _____, Esqs., out of the proceeds of the settlement for the claim of wrongful death, the sum of $ _____ as and for attorneys' fees, together with disbursements of $ _____, and

WD-2 (4/98)   - 4 -

WHY, the balance of the settlement, to wit the sum of $ _____, should not be distributed to those distributees having sustained a pecuniary loss as follows: _____% of the balance to _____, widow/widower of the decendent; _____% of the balance to _____, child of decedent; _____% of the balance to _____, child of the decedent, and

WHY the claim of the Department of Social Services in the amount of $ _____ should not be rejected, and

WHY the claim of _____ should not be rejected as a nondistributee, and

WHY the claim of _____, in the amount of $ _____ should not be rejected, and

WHY upon payments as hereinbefore mentioned by the said defendant, _____, or defendant's insurance company, the Insurance Company, the petitioner, as administrator of the goods, chattels and credits that were of _____, deceased, should not execute and deliver to the said defendant, _____, or defendant's Insurance Company a full, final and complete release in the claim against them arising out of the aforesaid cause of action together with any other papers necessary to effectuate said compromise.

Dated:

_____
Petitioner

_____ being duly sworn, deposes and says, that he/she is the petitioner in the within action, that he/she has read the foregoing petition and knows the contents thereof that the same is true of his/her own knowledge, except as to those matters therein stated to be alleged upon information and belief, and as to those matters he/she believes them to be true.

Sworn to before me this _____day of _____, 20___.

_____
Notary Public

Signature of New York Attorney:_____

Print Name of New York Attorney:_____

Firm Name: _____

Telephone Number:_____

Address of New York Attorney: _____

APPENDIX 12:
SAMPLE PETITION TO SETTLE A
WRONGFUL DEATH ACTION

ARIZONA FORM **Claim for Refund on Behalf of Deceased Taxpayer** **2002**
131

Refund claim for calendar year _____, or other tax year beginning ___/___/___, and ending ___/___/___.

PLEASE PRINT OR TYPE

1 Decedent's Name (last, first, middle initial)		2 Date of Death ___/___/___	3 Decedent's Social Security Number
4 Number and Street (permanent residence or domicile on date of death)		5 City, State, Zip Code	
6 Name of Person Claiming Refund (last, first, middle initial)	7 Relationship to Decedent	8 Claimant's Social Security or Federal I.D. Number	
9 Number and Street of Person Claiming Refund		10 City, State, Zip Code	

11 I am filing this claim as (check only one box):

   FOR DOR USE ONLY

a ☐ Surviving spouse claiming a refund based on a joint return

b ☐ Court Appointed Personal Representative for the decedent's estate. *Attach a court certificate showing your appointment.*

c ☐ Person other than 11a or 11b claiming refund for the decedent's estate. *Complete Schedule A below, and attach a copy of the death certificate or proof of death.*

Please attach requested information and sign below. If you checked box 11c, *complete Schedule A.*

[88]   [81]   [80]

SCHEDULE A *Complete only if you checked box (c) above.*

                YES   NO

12 Did the decedent leave a will? .... ☐ ☐

  A Has a personal representative been appointed for the estate of the decedent? .... ☐ ☐

  B If "No", will one be appointed? .... ☐ ☐
    If you answered "Yes" to 12a or 12b, do not file this form. The personal representative should file for the refund.

13 As the person claiming the refund for the decedent's estate, will you pay out the refund according to the laws of the state where the
decedent was a legal resident? .... ☐ ☐
If you answered "No", a refund cannot be made until you submit a court certificate showing your appointment as personal representative or
until you submit other evidence that you are entitled under state law to receive the refund.

I request a refund of taxes overpaid by, or on behalf of, the decedent. I, the undersigned claimant, certify under all penalties, fines and forfeitures imposed by law for the making of false or fraudulent claims against the State of Arizona or the making of false statements in connection therewith, that the statements made herein have been examined by me and that such statements are true to the best of my knowledge and belief.

Signature of Person Claiming Refund   Date

Instructions

· **Attach this form to the front of the income tax return that would have been filed if the decedent had lived.**

· If the refund is issued in the name of the decedent, it may be cashed with the endorsement of the executor or administrator of the estate.

· Attach any required documents, certificates, etc. to this form.

· For military personnel, the original or an authentic copy of a telegram or letter from the Department of Defense notifying the next of kin of the decedent's death while in active service, or a death certificate issued by the Department of Defense will be sufficient proof of death.

· As the surviving spouse or personal representative, you may be required to file a fiduciary return (Form 141) or an estate tax return (Form 72 or Form 76) for the decedent's estate. For further information concerning these forms, call (602) 255-3381, or toll-free from area codes 520 and 928, call (800) 352-4090.

APPENDIX 13:
ESTATE AND GIFT TAX EXEMPTIONS
(2002-2010)

YEAR	ESTATE TAX EXEMPTION	GIFT TAX EXEMPTION	HIGHEST ESTATE AND GIFT TAX RATE
2003	$1 million	$1 million	49%
2004	$1.5 million	$1 million	48%
2005	$1.5 million	$1 million	47%
2006	$2 million	$1 million	46%
2007	$2 million	$1 million	45%
2008	$2 million	$1 million	45%
2009	$3.5 million	$1 million	45%
2010	Estate tax repealed	$1 million	top individual income tax rate (gift tax only)

APPENDIX 14:
SAMPLE PETITION FOR JUDICIAL
SETTLEMENT OF AN ESTATE

DO NOT LEAVE ANY ITEMS BLANK

SURROGATE'S COURT OF THE STATE OF NEW YORK
COUNTY OF _____

---X

ACCOUNT BY

as the

of the ESTATE OF

a/k/a

Deceased.

---X

PETITION FOR JUDICIAL
SETTLEMENT OF ACCOUNT OF

[ ]   Executor
[ ]   Administrator
[ ]   Trustee
[ ]   Other [specify]

File No. _____

TO THE SURROGATE'S COURT, COUNTY OF _____

It is respectfully alleged:

1.   The name(s), and address(es) of the petitioner(s), the type and date of letters issued, and the
     amount and surety of petitioner's (s') bond, if any, are as follows:

Name: _____
Address: _____
            (Street Address)   (City/Town/Village)

_____
     (County)   (State)   (Zip)   (Telephone Number)

Mailing address: _____
                              (if different from above)

Type of letters issued: _____ Date letters issued: _____

Amount of bond: $ _____ Name of surety: _____

Name: _____
Address: _____
            (Street Address)   (City/Town/Village)

_____
     (County)   (State)   (Zip)   (Telephone Number)

Mailing address: _____
                              (if different from above)

Type of letters issued: _____ Date letters issued: _____

JA-1 (4/98)

---

2.   The decedent's name, date of death and domicile are as follows:

Name: _____ Date of death: _____
Domicile: _____
　　　　　　(Street Address)　　　　　　　　　　(City/Town/Village)

_____
　　　　　　(State)　　　　　　　　　　　　　　(Zip Code)

Township of: _____ County of: _____

3.   The petitioner(s) present (s) and render (s) herewith, a verified account of petitioner's (s') proceedings in this estate or trust, for the period from _____ to _____, showing the gross value of assets, including principal and income, to be the sum of $ _____.

4.   [ ]   (a)   An order was entered in this Court on _____, 20__.

[ ]   Exempting the estate from tax

[ ]   Fixing and assessing the tax due

[Attach a copy of the tax order and receipt]

[ ]   (b)   The following return (s) (was) (were) filled:

[ ]   ET-90 [For decedent's dying on or after May 25, 1990].

A copy was filed with the Surrogate's Court　　　[ ] Yes　　　[ ] No

[ ]   TT-385 [For decedent's dying before May 25, 1990]

[ ]   706 or 706NA

The estate taxes with respect to this estate were paid in full. [Attach a copy of letter of discharge.]

[ ]   (c)   No tax proceeding or return was required for this estate.

5.   The rendering of such account at this time is proper because check appropriate reason]

[ ]   seven months have elapsed since letters were issued to petitioner(s);

[ ]   letters issued to the petitioner(s) have been revoked,

[ ]   more than one year has elapsed since the preceding account of the petitioner(s) was settled;

[ ]   other reason [specify].

6.   The names and post-office addresses of all persons and parties interested in this proceeding who are required to be cited under the provisions of Surrogate's Court Procedure Act §2210, or otherwise, or concerning whom or which the Court is required to have information, are set forth in subdivision (a) or (b):

(a)   All persons and parties so interested herein who are of full age and sound mind, or which and sound mind, or which are corporations or associations, are as follows:

Name   Nature of Interest   P.O. Address

(b)   All persons so interested herein who are infants or incompetents or persons believed to be mentally incapable to adequately protect their rights, or persons whose existence, identity, or whereabouts are unknown (including persons who are virtually represented under SCPA §315) are as follows:

[Furnish all information specified in **NOTE** at bottom of page]

Name	Nature of Interest	P.O. Address

[NOTE: In the case of each infant, state   (a)   name, birth date, age, nature of interest, domicile, residence address, and the person with whom he/she resides;   (b)   whether or not he/she has a guardian or testamentary guardian, and whether or not his/her father, or if he/she be dead, his/her mother is living; and   (c) the name and post office address of any guardian and any living parent. In the case of each incompetent or person incapable of adequately protecting his/her rights, state   (a) name, nature of interest, and post office address;   (b) facts regarding his/her incompetency, including whether or not a committee has been appointed and whether or not he/she has been committed at any institution;   (c) the names and post office addresses of any committee, conservator, guardian, and person or institution having care and custody of him/her, and any relative or friend having an interest in his/her welfare. In the case of unknowns, describe in identical language to be used in citation for publication. In the case of a person confined as a prisoner, state place of incarceration. With respect to virtual representation see Uniform Court Rule, §207.18.]

7.   There are no persons interested in this proceeding other than those herein about mentioned.

8.   No prior application has been made to this or any other court for the relief requested in this petition.

        WHEREFORE the petitioner(s) pray (s) that the account of proceedings be judicially settled [specify any other relief requested.]

and that process be issued to all necessary parties who have not appeared to show cause why the relief requested should not be granted; and that an order be granted directing the service of process pursuant to the provisions of SCPA Article 3 upon such persons named in Paragraph (6) whose names or whereabouts are unknown and cannot be ascertained or who may be persons on whom service by personal delivery cannot be made.

Date: _____

1. _____   2. _____
        (Signature of Petitioner)   (Signature of Petitioner)

   _____   _____
        (Print Name)   (Print Name)

3. _____
        (Name of Corporate Petitioner)

   _____
        (Signature of Officer)

   _____
        (Print Name and Title of Officer)

VERIFICATION

[For use when petitioner is an individual]

STATE OF NEW YORK   )
COUNTY OF _____   ) ss.:

     The undersigned, the petitioner (s), named in the foregoing petition, being duly sworn, say (s): (I) (We) have read the foregoing petition subscribed by me (us) and know the contents thereof, and the same is true of (my) (our) own knowledge, except as to the matters therein stated to be alleged upon information and belief, and as to those matters (I) (we) believe it to be true.

_____   _____
(Signature of Petitioner)   (Signature of Petitioner)

_____   _____
(Print Name)   (Print Name)

Sworn to before me on
_____, 20__

Notary Public _____
Commission Expires:_____
(Affix Notary Stamp or Seal)

Signature of Attorney: _____
Print Name of Attorney: _____
Firm Name: _____
Tel. No.: _____
Address of Attorney: _____
_____
_____

VERIFICATION

[For use when petitioner is a bank or trust company]

STATE OF NEW YORK   )
COUNTY OF _____) ss.:

I, the undersigned, a _____ of
                                  (Title)

_____
             (Name of Bank or Trust Company)
being duly sworn, say (s),

      I have read the foregoing petition subscribed by me and know the contents thereof, and the same is true of my own knowledge, except as to the matters stated to be alleged upon information and belief, and as to those matters I believe it to be true.

_____
(Name of Bank or Trust)

BY _____
       (Signature of Officer)

_____
(Print Name and Title)

Sworn to before me on
_____, 20___

Notary Public _____
Commission Expires:_____
(Affix Notary Stamp or Seal)

Signature of Attorney: _____
Print Name of Attorney: _____
Firm Name: _____
Tel. No.: _____
Address of Attorney: _____
_____
_____

SURROGATE'S COURT OF THE STATE OF NEW YORK
COUNTY OF
--X
ACCOUNTING BY

as the

of the ESTATE OF

a/k/a

Deceased
--X

ACCOUNTING BY:

[ ]   Executor
[ ]   Trustee
[ ]   Other [Specify]_____

File No. _____

TO THE SURROGATE'S COURT OF THE COUNTY OF
    The undersigned does hereby render the account of proceedings as follows:

    Period of account from _____ to _____
    This is a (final) (intermediate) account. [delete inapplicable term]

    [The instructions concerning the schedules need not be stated at the head of each schedule. It will be sufficient to set forth only the schedule letter and heading. For convenience of reference, the schedule letter and page number of the schedule should be shown at the bottom of each sheet of the account.]

Schedule A   -   Principal Received, page _____
Schedule A-1-   Realized Increases, page _____
Schedule B   -   Realized Decreases, page _____
Schedule C   -   Funeral and Administration Expenses and Taxes, page _____
Schedule C-1 -   Unpaid Administration Expenses, page _____
Schedule D   -   Creditor's Claims, page _____
Schedule E   -   Distributions Made, page _____
Schedule F   -   New Investments, Exchanges and Stock Distribution, page _____
Schedule G   -   Personal Property Remaining on Hand, page _____
Schedule H   -   Interested Parties and Proposed Distribution, page _____
Schedule I   -   Computation of Commissions, page _____
Schedule J   -   Other Pertinent Facts and Cash Reconciliation, page _____
Schedule K   -   Estate Taxes Paid and Allocation of Estate Taxes, page _____

JA-7 (6/98)

SUMMARY

CHARGES:

Schedule "A"	-	(Principal received)	$ _____
Schedule "A - 1"	-	(Realized increases in principal)	$ _____
Schedule "A - 2"	-	(Income Collected)	$ _____
Total charges			$ _____

CREDITS:

Schedule "B"	-	(Realized decreases in principal)	$ _____
Schedule "C"	-	(Funeral and administration expenses)	$ _____
Schedule "D"	-	(Creditor's claims actually paid)	$ _____
Schedule "E"	-	(Distributions of principal)	$ _____
Total credits			$ _____
Balance on hand shown by Schedule "G"			$ _____

The foregoing balance of $ _____ consists of $ _____ in cash and $ _____ in other property on hand as of the _____ day of _____, 20__. It is subject to deduction of estimated principal commissions amounting to $ _____ as shown in Schedule I, and to the proper charge to principal of expenses of this accounting.

The attached schedules are part of this account.

_____
(Name of Corporate Fiduciary)

_____
(Signature of Fiduciary)

_____
(Signature of Officer)

_____
(Signature of Fiduciary)

AFFIDAVIT OF ACCOUNTING PARTY

STATE OF NEW YORK)
COUNTY OF) ss.:

_____ being duly sworn, says: that the schedules of assets of the estate reported herein are true and complete and include all money and property of any kind, and all increment thereon, which have come into the hands of any of the accounting parties or have been received by any other persons for the use of any accounting party by order of authority of such accounting party, and include all indebtedness due by any accounting party to the estate whether discharged or not; that the moneys stated in the account as collected were all that could be collected; that all claims for credit for losses or decreases of value of assets are correctly reported; that the reported payments out of estate assets for funeral and administration expenses were actually made and made in the amounts scheduled; that the reported payments to creditors and beneficiaries were actually made at the dates and in the amounts scheduled; that no payments have been made by any accounting party on any fiduciary's claims against the estate except after prior approval and allowance by the Surrogate; that all receipts and disbursements are correctly and fully reported and scheduled; that the accounting parties do not know of any error in the account or in any schedule thereof or of any matter or thing relating to the estate omitted therefrom to the prejudice of rights of any creditor or of any person interested in the estate; and that the schedule of commissions has been computed in conformity with the statute regulating commissions and the Rules of the Surrogate's Court applicable thereto.

Sworn to before me on
_____, 20____   _____
                                                            Signature

_____   _____
Notary Public   Print Name
Commission Expires:
(Affix Notary Stamp or Seal)

Signature of Attorney: _____ Tel. No.: _____
Address of Attorney: _____
_____

INSTRUCTIONS
PRINCIPAL

Schedule A

Statement of Principal Received

This schedule must contain an itemized statement of all the moneys and other personal property constituting principal for which each accounting party is charged, together with the date of receipt or acquisition of such money or property. If real property has been sold by the fiduciary, this schedule must set forth the proceeds of sale of such property, including a copy of the closing statement.

Schedule A-1

Statement of Increases on Sales, Liquidation or Distribution

This schedule must contain a full and complete statement of all realized increases derived from principal assets whether due to sale, liquidation, or distribution or any other reason. It should also show realized increases on new investments or exchanges. In each instance, the date of realization of the increase must be shown and the property from which the increase was derived must be identified.

Schedule A-2

Statement of All Income Collected

This schedule must contain a full and complete statement of all interest, dividends, rents and other income received, and the date of each receipt. Each receipt must be separately accounted for and identified, except that where a security had been held for an entire year, the interest or ordinary dividends may be reported on a calendar year basis.

Schedule B

Statement of Decreases Due to Sales, Liquidation, Collection, Distribution or Uncollectibility

This schedule must contain a full and complete statement of all realized decreases on principal assets whether due to sale, liquidation, collection or distribution, or any other reason. It should show decreases on new investments or exchanges and also sales, liquidations or distributions that result in neither gain nor loss. In each instance, the date of realization of the decrease must be shown and the property from which the decrease was incurred must be identified. It should also report any asset which the fiduciary intends to abandon as worthless, together with a full statement of the reasons for abandoning it.

Schedule C

Statement of Funeral and Administration Expenses and Taxes Charged to Principal

This schedule must contain an itemized statement of all moneys chargeable and paid for funeral, administration and other necessary expenses, together with the date and the reason for each expenditure. Consolidate all similar expenditures; i.e. funeral expenses, taxes, accountant fees, legal fees, filing fees, commissions, other. Where the will directs that all inheritance and death taxes are to be paid out of the estate, credit for payment of the same should be taken in this schedule.

Schedule C-1

Statement of Unpaid Administration Expenses

This schedule must contain an itemized statement of all unpaid claims for administration and other necessary expenses, together with a statement of the basis for each such claim.

Schedule D

Statement of All Creditor's Claims

This schedule must contain an itemized statement of all creditor's claims subdivided to show:

1. Claims presented, allowed, paid and credited and appearing in the Summary Statement together with the date of payment.
2. Claims presented and allowed but not paid.
3. Claims presented but rejected, and the date of and the reason for such rejection.
4. Contingent and possible claims.
5. Personal claims requiring approval by the court pursuant to SCPA §1805.

In the event of insolvency, preference of various claims should be stated, with the order of their priority.

Schedule E

Statement of Distributions of Principal

This schedule must contain an itemized statement of all moneys paid and all property delivered from principal to the beneficiaries, legatees, trustees, surviving spouse or distributees of the deceased, the date of payment or delivery thereof, and the name of the person to whom payment or delivery was actually made.

Where estate taxes are required to be apportioned and payments have been made on account of the taxes, the amounts apportioned in Schedule K against beneficiaries of the estate shall be charged against the respective individuals share.

Schedule F

Statement of New Investments, Exchanges and Stock Distributions

This schedule must contain an itemized statement of (a) all new investments made by the fiduciary with the date of acquisition and cost of all property purchased, (b) all exchanges made by the fiduciary, specifying dates and items received and items surrendered, and (c) all stock dividends, stock splits, right and warrants received by the fiduciary, showing the securities to which each relates and their allocation as between principal and income.

Schedule G

Statement of Principal Remaining on Hand

This schedule must contain an itemized statement showing all property constituting principal remaining on hand including a statement of all uncollected receivables and property rights due to the estate. Show the date and cost of all such property that was acquired by purchase, exchange or transfers made or received, together with the date of acquisition and the cost thereof and indicate such sums in the appropriate lines of the summary schedule. Show all unrealized increases and decreases relating to assets on hand, and report the same in the appropriate places in the summary schedule.

Schedule H

Statement of Interested Parties

This schedule must contain the names of all persons entitled as beneficiary, legatee, devisee, trustee, surviving spouse, distributee, unpaid creditor or otherwise to a share of the estate or fund, with their post office addresses and the degree of relationship, if any, of each to the deceased, and a statement showing the nature of and the value or approximate value of the interest of each such person.

This schedule also must contain a statement that the records of this court have been searched for powers of attorney and assignments and encumbrances made and executed by any of the persons interested in or entitled to a share of the estate and a list detailing each power of attorney, assignment and encumbrance, disclosed by such search, with the date of its recording and the name and address of each attorney in fact and of each assignee and of each person beneficially interested under the encumbrance to in the respective instruments, and also whether the accounting party had any knowledge of the execution of any such power of attorney or assignment not so filed and recorded.

Schedule I

Statement of Computation of Commissions

This schedule must contain a computation of the amount of commissions due upon this accounting. See Uniform Court Rule, §207.40 (d).

Schedule J

Statement of Other Pertinent Facts, and Cash Reconciliation

This schedule must contain a statement of all other pertinent facts affecting the administration of the estate and the rights of those interested therein. It must also contain a statement of any real property left by the decedent that it is not necessary to include as an estate asset to be accounted for, a brief description thereof, its gross value, and the amount of mortgages or liens thereon at the date of death of the deceased. A cash reconciliation must also be set forth in this schedule so that verification with bank statements and cash on hand may be readily made.

Schedule K

Statement of Estate Taxes Paid and Allocation Thereof

This schedule must contain a statement showing all estate taxes assessed and paid with respect to any property required to be included in the gross estate of the decedent under the provisions of the Tax Law or under the laws of the United States. This schedule must also contain a computation setting forth the proposed allocation of taxes paid and to be paid and the amounts due the estate from each person in whose behalf a tax payment has been made and also the proportionate amount of the tax paid by each of the named persons interested in this estate or charged against their respective interest, as provided in §2-1.8 of the Estates, Powers and Trusts Law.

Where an allocation of taxes is required, the method of computing the allocation of said taxes must be shown in this schedule.

SURROGATE'S COURT OF THE STATE OF NEW YORK

COUNTY OF

--X

ACCOUNTING BY   RECEIPT AND RELEASE

as the

of the ESTATE OF   File No. _____

a/k/a   Deceased

--X

     The undersigned, being of full age, sound mind and under no disability, and entitled to share in the estate of the above named decedent as a   [check one]   [ ] legatee under a will,   [ ] distributee of an intestate share,   [ ] trust beneficiary, [ ] creditor of the estate,   [ ] other [specify] _____

    (a) Acknowledges that each fiduciary named above has fully and satisfactorily accounted for all assets of the estate;

    (b) Approves the written account verified on _____, 20__ as submitted to the undersigned; [Delete paragraphs (a) and (b) if the undersigned is not interested in or affected by the amount of the residuary estate or trust, or if being made pursuant to a decree of the court.]

    (c) Acknowledges receipt of money paid or property transferred or delivered as follows:

            money (cash or check): $ _____

            the following property: valued at $ _____

    The following payment and/or transfer is in full payment or distribution of :

    [ ] a legacy under Paragraph/Article _____ of the will or trust;
    [ ] a claim against the estate;
    [ ] the amount directed to be paid by a decree of this court dated: _____, 20__
    [ ] other [specify]: _____

    (d) Releases and discharges each fiduciary named above from all liability to the undersigned for any and all matters relating to or derived from the administration of the estate; waives the issuance and service of a citation to attend any and all proceedings for the judicial settlement of the account; and authorizes the Surrogate to make and enter a decree settling the account and fully releasing and discharging each fiduciary named above as to all matters embraced therein.

Dated: _____

_____   _____
      (Signature)   (Corporate Name)

_____   _____
      (Print Name)   (Signature of Officer)

JA-2 (12/96)

STATE OF NEW YORK   )
COUNTY OF   )   ss.:

On _____. 20___, before me personally appeared [INDIVIDUAL] _____

[ ] _____ to me known and known to me to be the person described in and who
executed the foregoing receipt and release and duly acknowledged the execution thereof.

[CORPORATION] _____

[ ] _____ to me known, who duly swore to the foregoing instrument and
who did say that he/she resides at _____ and that he/she is a
_____ of _____ the corporation/national
banking association described in and which executed such instrument; and that he/she signed his/her name
thereto by order of the Board of Directors of the corporation.

Sworn to before me on
_____, 20____

_____
Signature

_____
Notary Public
Commission Expires:
(Affix Notary Stamp or Seal)

_____
Print Name

Signature of Attorney: _____ Tel. No.: _____
Address of Attorney: _____
_____

SURROGATE'S COURT OF THE STATE OF NEW YORK
COUNTY OF
--X
ACCOUNTING BY   WAIVER OF CITATION AND CONSENT
                                                        IN ACCOUNTING
as the

of the ESTATE OF   File No _____

a/k/a   Deceased.
--X

    The undersigned, being of full age, and sound mind, residing at the address written below, having an interest in this proceeding, waives the issuance and service of citation in this proceeding, and consents to the submission of a decree settling the account as filed and adjusted without further notice. I acknowledge receipt of a copy of the summary statement of account.

Date	Signature	Street Address	Interest

Print Name	City/Town/Village	State/Zip

STATE OF NEW YORK   )
COUNTY OF   ) ss.:

    On _____, 20___, before me personally appeared [INDIVIDUAL] _____
to me know and known to me to be the person described in and who executed the foregoing waiver and consent and duly acknowledged the execution thereof.

[CORPORATION] _____ to me know, who duly swore to the foregoing instrument and who did say that he/she resides at _____ and that he/she is a _____ of _____the corporation/national banking association described in and which executed such instrument; and that he/she signed his/her name by order of the Board of Directors of the corporation.

Sworn to before me on
_____, 20____   _____
                                           Signature

_____   _____
Notary Public   Print Name
Commission Expires:
(Affix Notary Stamp or Seal)

Signature of Attorney: _____ Tel. No.: _____
Address of Attorney: _____
_____

[Note: You may request a copy of the full account from the petitioner or petitioner's attorney.]

JA-3 (12/96)

ACCOUNTING CITATION   File No. _____

SURROGATE'S COURT - _____ COUNTY

CITATION

THE PEOPLE OF THE STATE OF NEW YORK,
By the Grace of God Free and Independent

TO

A petition and an account having been duly filed by _____,

whose address is _____

_____

YOU ARE HEREBY CITED TO SHOW CAUSE before the Surrogate's Court, _____ County,

at _____, New York, on _____ 20___, at _____ o'clock in the _____ noon of

that day, why the account of _____, a summary of which has been served herewith,

as of the estate of _____ should not be judicially settled.

[State any further relief requested]

Dated, Attested and Sealed.

HON. _____, Surrogate

_____, 20__

(Seal)   Chief Clerk

Name of Attorney: _____   Tel. No.: _____

Address of Attorney: _____

_____

[Note: This citation is served upon you as required by law. You are not required to appear; however, if you fail to appear it will
be assumed you do not object to the relief requested. You have a right to have an attorney appear for you, and you or your
attorney may request a copy of the full account from the petitioner or petitioner's attorney.]

JA-6   (12/96)

SURROGATE'S COURT OF THE STATE OF NEW YORK
COUNTY OF
---X

ACCOUNTING BY	FINAL/INTERMEDIATE
	DECREE OF JUDICIAL SETTLEMENT
as the	EXECUTOR WITH TRUST OR TRUSTEE
of the ESTATE OF	File No. _____
a/k/a	
Deceased.	

---X

A petition praying for a decree judicially settling the final/intermediate account having been presented and filed in this court and the time to present claims against the estate having expired, and a citation having been issued directed to all persons interested in this proceeding requiring them to show cause why a decree should not be granted judicially settling the account prayed for in the petition, and the citation having been returned with proof of due service thereof on the following:

and duly executed waivers of the service of citation or receipts and releases having been filed for the following:

and the following parties having appeared in answer to the citation:

and _____, attorneys, having appeared for the petitioner, and there being no other appearances; and the Surrogate having appointed _____ as _____ guardian ad litem for the following persons under a disability:

and each guardian ad litem having filed a report recommending that the account be judicially settled and no objection having been filed to the account;

and it appearing that all tax returns required by law have been filed and all New York State estate taxes have been fully paid, provision made therefore, or the estate is exempt from tax; and the Surrogate having examined the account and having found that each petitioner has fully accounted for all of the monies and property of the estate that have come into the petitioner's hands for the period of the account, as adjusted, it is

ORDERED, ADJUDGED AND DECREED, that the final/intermediate account be and the same hereby is judicially settled and allowed as filed (and adjusted), and that the following is a summary thereof as settled:

SUMMARY

PRINCIPAL ACCOUNT

CHARGES:

Schedule "A"	-	(Principal received)	$ _____
Schedule "A - 1"	-	(Realized increases in principal)	$ _____
Schedule "A-2"	-	(Income Collected)	$ _____
Total Charges			$ _____

CREDITS:

Schedule "B"	-	(Realized decreases in principal)	$ _____
Schedule "C"	-	(Funeral and administration expenses)	$ _____
Schedule "D"	-	(Creditor's claims actually paid)	$ _____
Schedule "E"	-	(Distributions of principal)	$ _____
Total Credits			$ _____
Balance on hand shown by Schedule "G"			$ _____

and it is further

ORDERED, ADJUDGED AND DECREED, that petitioner(s) pay the remaining cash and transfer, assign and deliver the other remaining assets as shown in the account as follows:

To the petitioner:
as and for commissions the sum of $ _____ :

To the petitioner:
as and for commissions the sum of $ _____ :

To the attorney:
for legal services rendered for
the benefit of the estate the sum of $ _____ :

and for costs and disbursements
(which sums are in addition to any payments
made on account and allowed by the court) $ _____ :

To the guardian ad litem:
for services as guardian ad litem $ _____ :

and it is further

ORDERED, ADJUDGED AND DECREED, that the balance remaining on hand in the amount of $ _____ be paid as follows:

To: _____ $ _____

ORDERED, ADJUDGED AND DECREED, that upon complying with the directions of this decree and the filing of the receipts for the payments herein directed, the petitioner (s) hereby shall be discharged as to all matters and things contained in this accounting and decree.

Dated: _____   _____
                                        Judge of the Surrogate's Court

APPENDIX 15:
SAMPLE ORDER OF FINAL DISCHARGE

CC-26   **District Court**
                        CLARK COUNTY, NEVADA

In the Matter of the Estate of

                                    CASE NO. _____

                    Deceased.   **ORDER OF FINAL DISCHARGE**

     The Court being advised that in accordance with the Order of Distribution and as evidenced by the attached exhibits, the Estate of the Decedent has been fully administered, that all sums of money have been paid, that all property of the Estate has been delivered, that all other acts lawfully required have been performed, now good cause appearing, it is hereby

     ORDERED that _____, who has fully and faithfully performed the duties of _____ of the Estate of the Decedent, is discharged from all further duties and responsibilities, that the Letters _____ _____are vacated, that the Estate is declared to be fully distributed, settled and closed and that the sureties are released and the bond, if any, is exonerated from all liabilities hereafter incurred.

     DATED this _____ day of _____, _____.

                        _____
                                DISTRICT COURT JUDGE
Submitted By:

_____
                 (SIGNATURE)
Name _____
Address: _____
City/State/Zip: _____
Telephone: _____
Attorney for: _____   REV6/01/cc

APPENDIX 16:
SAMPLE APPLICATION FOR VA
DEATH BENEFITS

 **Department of
Veterans Affairs**

APPLICATION FOR DEPENDENCY AND INDEMNITY COMPENSATION, DEATH
PENSION AND ACCRUED BENEFITS BY A SURVIVING SPOUSE OR CHILD
(INCLUDING DEATH COMPENSATION IF APPLICABLE)
VA FORM NUMBER 21-534

A. QUESTIONS? GET FREE INFORMATION: If you have any questions about this form,
how to fill it out, or need information about other Department of Veterans Affairs (VA)
benefits, call us:

VA NATIONWIDE TOLL-FREE NUMBER:

1 -800 -827 -1000

(Hearing Impaired—TDD 1-800-829-4833)

B. YOU SHOULD USE THIS FORM TO:

(1) Apply for VA benefits you may be entitled to receive as a surviving spouse or child of a
deceased veteran;

(2) Apply for any money VA owes the veteran but did not pay prior to death (called accrued
benefits):

(3) If you apply for any one of these benefits, the law requires that we also consider you for the
others.

(4) SOCIAL SECURITY BENEFITS: You can apply for Social Security (SS) benefits now by using
the SSA-24 attached to this VA Form. (See pages 11 and 12.) You don't have to apply if you don't
want to or if you already have. If you do want to apply, fill it out and leave it attached. We will send
it to the Social Security Administration. They will then contact you.

C. WHEN YOU ARE DONE WITH THIS FORM: Mail it or take it to a VA Regional Office.

D. REGIONAL OFFICE ADDRESS: You should call the VA toll-free number, 1-800-827-1000, for the
address or location of the Regional Office. You might find that office's address in the blue pages of
your telephone book. It may be under "United States Government, Veterans Affairs."

IMPORTANT

E. PLEASE BEGIN BY FOLLOWING THE DETAILED INSTRUCTIONS. They begin on page 2.

F. PRINT ALL ANSWERS CLEARLY. If you must write the answers do so very clearly and plainly. If
an answer is "None" or "O", write that. YOUR ANSWER TO EVERY QUESTION IS IMPORTANT to
help us complete your claim.

G. YOU MUST SIGN AND DATE this application at the bottom of page 9.

H. MAKE A PHOTOCOPY OF THIS APPLICATION for your records before you mail it. Also, tear off
and keep this instruction page and all other separate instruction pages.

VA FORM 21-534
JUN 1998

PAGE 1

INSTRUCTIONS FOR VA FORM 21-534

READ VERY CAREFULLY, DETACH, AND RETAIN THESE INSTRUCTION SHEETS FOR YOUR REFERENCE

CALL VA AT 1 800 827 1000 FOR FREE HELP WITH THIS FORM (HEARING IMPAIRED TDD 1 800 829 4833)

A. PAYMENT OF BENEFITS - GENERAL

(1) Dependency and Indemnity Compensation may be payable when (1) the veteran's death occurred in service, or (2) when a veteran dies of service-connected disability, or (3) in certain circumstances if a veteran rated totally disabled from service-connected disability dies from non-service-connected conditions.

(2) Death Pension may be payable when the death of a veteran with wartime service is not due to service, provided income is within applicable limits.

(3) A higher rate of benefits is payable to a surviving spouse who is a patient in a nursing home or otherwise determined to be in need of regular aid and attendance or who is permanently housebound due to disability.

(a) The rate of pension paid depends upon the amount of family income and the number of dependent children, according to a formula provided by law.

(b) If there is no surviving spouse, pension may be payable on behalf of a child or children.

(c) Because benefit rates and income limits are frequently changed, it is not possible to keep such information current in these instructions. Information regarding current income limitations and rates of benefits may be obtained by contacting your nearest VA office at 1 800 827 1000.

(4) Unless a claim for Dependency and Indemnity Compensation is filed within one year from date of death, that benefit is not payable from a date earlier than the date the claim is received in the VA.

(5) Unless a claim for pension is filed within 45 days from date of death, that benefit is not payable from a date earlier than the date the claim is received in the VA.

B. REPRESENTATION - You may be represented, without charge, by an accredited representative of a veterans organization or other service organization, recognized by the Secretary of the Veterans Affairs, or you may employ an attorney to assist you with your claim. Typical examples of counsel who may be available include attorneys in private practice or legal aid services. If you desire representation, let us know and we will send you the necessary forms. If you have already designated a representative, no further action is required on your part.

C. HEARINGS - You have the right to a personal hearing at any stage of claims processing, either before or after a decision is made. This right may be exercised with regard to an original claim, supplemental claim or with regard to any subsequent action affecting your entitlement. All you need do is inform the nearest VA office as to your desires, and we will arrange a time and place for the hearing. You may bring witnesses if you desire and their testimony will be entered in the record. VA will furnish the hearing room, provide hearing officials, and prepare the transcript of the proceedings. VA cannot pay any of your expenses in connection with the hearing.

D. HOW TO COMPLETE THE APPLICATION - ALL THE INFORMATION REQUESTED MUST BE ANSWERED FULLY AND CLEARLY OR ACTION ON YOUR CLAIM MAY BE DELAYED. IF YOU DO NOT KNOW THE ANSWER, WRITE "UNKNOWN."

E. MINORS AND INCOMPETENTS - If the person for whom the claim is being made is a minor or is incompetent, the application form should be completed and filed by the legal guardian or, if no legal guardian has been appointed, it may be completed and filed by some person acting on behalf of the minor or incompetent.

F. EVIDENCE - GENERAL - If you are unable to furnish with this application form any of the required evidence asked for anywhere in these instructions, state why you are unable on a separate sheet. Evidence filed previously with the Department of Veterans Affairs need not be filed again in connection with this claim at this time.

G. EVIDENCE - MEDICAL - A medical statement should accompany the application of a surviving spouse who is housebound or who requires the aid and attendance of another person if he or she is not a nursing home patient. A nursing home patient should furnish a statement signed by an official of the nursing home showing the date of admission and patient status. Also, indicate in Item 37, "Remarks," that you are a nursing home patient and give the name and address of the nursing home.

PAGE 2

H. SERVICE INFORMATION (See application form, Part I, blocks 11A, 11B, 11C and 11D) - Complete information should be furnished for each period of the veteran's active service including service as a commissioned officer in the National Oceanic and Atmospheric Administration including officers of the Coast and Geodetic Survey and Environmental Science Services Administration or Public Health Service. If the veteran never filed a claim with the Department of Veterans Affairs, you should furnish the discharge or separation document issued by the service department for each period of service listed.

I. INFORMATION RELATING TO MARRIAGE (See application form Part II) - Complete information concerning all marriages entered into by either the surviving spouse or the veteran and the termination of such marriages must be furnished in Items 13 through 17. Specific details as to date, place and manner of dissolution of each marriage must be included. Show the month, day and year for "date". Show city and state for "place".

J. INFORMATION CONCERNING CHILDREN (See application form Part III)

(1) PROOF OF AGE AND RELATIONSHIP OF CHILD. Complete information concerning the birth of all children of the veteran must be furnished in Items 22 through 24. Show the month, day and year for "date." Show city and state for "place."

(2) HELPLESS CHILD. If any child is claimed as being permanently incapable of self-support by reason of mental or physical defect, it must be shown that such incapacity existed prior to the date the child attained age 18. The nature and extent of the physical or mental impairment should be shown by a statement from the attending physician or other medical evidence, forwarded with the application.

K. NET WORTH (See application form, Part IV)

(1) MINORS AND INCOMPETENTS.

(a) Custodian or Guardian of a Surviving Spouse - Report only the net worth of your ward.

(b) Custodian of Child(ren) - Report your net worth as well as the individual net worth of EACH CHILD for whom benefits are claimed.

(2) SURVIVING SPOUSE WITH CHILDREN. When a surviving spouse files application in his/her own right, the separate net worth of each child for whom benefits are claimed must also be reported.

(3) CHILDREN ALONE. When application is filed on behalf of a child in his or her own right, the child's net worth should be reported.

Item 25A - Include market value of stocks, checking accounts, bank deposits, savings and loan accounts, cash and currency.

Item 25B - Do not include the value of the single dwelling unit or that portion of real property used solely as your principal residence. On all other real estate reduce the market value by amount of any money owed on it such as mortgages or other indebtedness.

Item 25C - Report the total market value of all rights and interest in all other property not included in Items 25A and B. "Market value" is the price it would currently receive if sold in an open market. Do not include value of ordinary personal effects necessary for your daily living such as an automobile, clothing, furniture and the dwelling (single family unit) used as your principal residence.

Item 25D - Report the total of Items 25A through 25C. This should be your net worth.

L. INCOME OF SURVIVING SPOUSE AND/OR CHILD(REN) (See application form, Part V)

(1) MINORS AND INCOMPETENTS.

(a) Custodian or Guardian of a Surviving Spouse - Report only the income of your ward.

(b) Custodian of Child(ren) - Report your income as well as the individual income of each child for whom benefits are claimed.

(2) SURVIVING SPOUSE WITH CHILDREN. When a surviving spouse files application in his/her right, the separate income of each child for whom benefits are claimed must also be reported.

PAGE 3

(3) FOREIGN CURRENCY EXCHANGE RATES. If you report income in foreign currency, we will convert it into dollars based on the average exchange rate for the preceding four quarters (as provided by the Department of the Treasury).

IMPORTANT

YOU MUST SHOW ALL TYPES OF PAYMENTS AND INCOMES FROM ALL SOURCES FOR YOURSELF, SPOUSE AND DEPENDENT CHILDREN BEFORE ANY DEDUCTIONS OR WITHHOLDINGS. UNDER 38 CFR 3.271(a), PAYMENTS OF ANY KIND FROM ANY SOURCE SHALL BE COUNTED AS INCOME UNLESS SPECIFICALLY EXCLUDED BY LAW. VA WILL DETERMINE ANY AMOUNT WHICH DOES NOT COUNT. INCLUDE ALL SEVERANCE PAY OR OTHER ACCRUED PAYMENTS OF ANY KIND OR FROM ANY SOURCE. WHEN NO INCOME IS RECEIVED OR EXPECTED FROM A SPECIFIED SOURCE, WRITE "NONE" IN THE APPROPRIATE BLOCK (ITEMS 26C THROUGH 28D). IF INCOME FROM ANY SOURCE IS ANTICIPATED BUT THE AMOUNT IS NOT YET DETERMINED, WRITE "UNDETERMINED" IN THE APPROPRIATE BLOCK. ATTACH SEPARATE SHEETS IF ADDITIONAL SPACE IS NEEDED.

Items 27F and 28D - When income is reported in these items, the source must be shown in "Remarks," Item 37. If that income is from two or more sources, list each amount separately and clearly indicate the source.

M. COURT OR CLAIM JUDGEMENT, SETTLEMENTS OR COMPROMISES. Money or property received as a result of a claim or legal action for damages based upon the death of the veteran may affect payment of Dependency and Indemnity Compensation or Pension. You must report whether a claim or court action is pending or whether a court decree or settlement or compromise of a claim for damages has been made.

N. DEDUCTIBLE EXPENSES (See application form, Part VI)

(1) If you have paid any expenses of last illness and burial or just debts of the veteran, report them in Part VI of the application. You should also report any expenses of last illness and burial of any children of the veteran, if applicable. Report only payments for which you will not be reimbursed. If you receive reimbursement after you have filed this claim, promptly advise the VA office handling your claim.

(2) Family medical expenses and educational or vocational rehabilitation expenses paid by you may affect your rate of pension. You should report these expenses at the end of the year.

(3) If you expect to have a continuing high level of unreimbursed medical expenses throughout the year (such as nursing home fees), please make a statement to that effect in "Remarks," Item 37.

PRIVACY ACT INFORMATION: No allowance of compensation or pension may be granted unless this form is completed fully as required by existing law (38 U.S.C. Chapters 13 and 15, Subchapter III). The responses you submit are considered confidential (38 U.S.C. 5701). They may be disclosed outside VA only if the disclosure is authorized under the Privacy Act, including the routine uses identified in the VA system of records, 58VA21/22, Compensation, Pension, Education and Rehabilitation Records - VA, published in the Federal Register. The requested information is considered relevant and necessary to determine maximum benefits under the law. Information submitted is subject to verification through computer matching programs with other agencies.

Income information and employment information furnished by you will be compared with information obtained by VA from the Secretary of Health and Human Services or the Secretary of the Treasury under clause (viii) of section 6103(1)(7)(D) of the Internal Revenue Code of 1986. Any information provided by you including your Social Security Number, may be used in matching programs conducted in connection with any proceeding for the collection of an amount owed the United States by virtue of your participation in any benefit program administered by the Department of Veterans Affairs.

RESPONDENT BURDEN: VA may not conduct or sponsor, and respondent is not required to respond to this collection of information unless it displays a valid OMB Control Number. Public reporting burden for this collection of information is estimated to average 1 hour and 15 minutes per response, including the time for reviewing instructions, searching existing data sources, gathering and maintaining the data needed, and completing and reviewing the collection of information. If you have comments regarding this burden estimate or any other aspect of this collection of information, call 1-800-827-1000 for mailing information on where to send your comments

OMB Approved NO 2900 0004
Respondent Burden: 1 hour 15 minutes

Department of Veterans Affairs

(DO NOT WRITE IN THIS SPACE)
VA DATE STAMP

APPLICATION FOR DEPENDENCY AND INDEMNITY COMPENSATION, DEATH PENSION AND ACCRUED BENEFITS BY A SURVIVING SPOUSE OR CHILD (INCLUDING DEATH COMPENSATION IF APPLICABLE)

IMPORTANT - Read instructions carefully before completing this form. Answer all items fully. Detach and retain ONLY the instruction sheets. If more space is required, attach additional sheets and identify each answer by item number. Write clearly or print the answers.

1. NAME OF DECEASED VETERAN (First, middle, last)	2. VA FILE NO.
	XC/XSS

3. IF VETERAN PREVIOUSLY APPLIED TO THE VA FOR ANY BENEFIT INSERT VA FILE NUMBER, IF KNOWN, AND IF DIFFERENT FROM ITEM 2	4. RAILROAD RETIREMENT	5. SOCIAL SECURITY NO. OF VETERAN

6A. NAME OF CLAIMANT (First, middle, last)	6B. DAYTIME TELEPHONE NO. (Include Area Code)

6C. MAILING ADDRESS OF CLAIMANT (No.and street or rural route, City or P.O.,State and ZIP) Code)	6D. RELATIONSHIP TO VETERAN (Check One)
	☐ SURVIVING SPOUSE ☐ CHILD
	6E. SOCIAL SECURITY NO. OF SURVIVING SPOUSE OR CLAIMANT

PART I - IDENTIFICATION AND SERVICE INFORMATION OF VETERAN (See Instructions, Paragraph H)

7. DATE OF BIRTH	8. DATE OF DEATH	9. PLACE OF DEATH

10. ARE YOU CLAIMING THAT THE CAUSE OF DEATH WAS DUE TO SERVICE?
☐ YES   ☐ NO

11A. ENTERED ACTIVE SERVICE		11B. SERVICE NO.	11C. SEPARATED FROM ACTIVE SERVICE		11D. GRADE,RANK OR RATING, ORGANIZATION AND BRANCH OF SERVICE
DATE	PLACE		DATE	PLACE	

12. IF VETERAN SERVED UNDER A NAME OTHER THAN THAT SHOWN IN ITEM 1, GIVE THAT FULL NAME, SERVICE DATES AND BRANCH OF SERVICE USING THAT NAME

PART II - INFORMATION RELATING TO MARRIAGE (See Instructions, Paragraph I)

INFORMATION RELATING TO VETERAN

13. HOW MANY TIMES WAS VETERAN MARRIED?

NOTE: Where a date is requested, show month, day, and year. Where a place is requested, show city and state.

14A. MARRIAGE		14B. TO WHOM MARRIED	14C. HOW MARRIAGE ENDED (Death, divorce, etc.)	14D. MARRIAGE ENDED	
DATE	PLACE			DATE	PLACE

INFORMATION RELATING TO SURVIVING SPOUSE

NOTE: If claimant is not veteran's surviving spouse, omit items 15 to 21 inclusive.

15. HOW MANY TIMES HAS SURVIVING SPOUSE BEEN MARRIED?	16. HAS SURVIVING SPOUSE REMARRIED SINCE DEATH OF VETERAN? ☐ YES ☐ NO

NOTE: Where a date is requested, show month, day, and year. Where a place is requested, show city and state.

17A. MARRIAGE		17B. TO WHOM MARRIED	17C. HOW MARRIAGE ENDED (Death, divorce, etc.)	17D. MARRIAGE ENDED	
DATE	PLACE			DATE	PLACE

YOU MUST SIGN AND DATE THIS FORM AT THE BOTTOM OF PAGE 9.

VA FORM
JUN 1998 21 -534

EXISTING STOCK OF VA FORM 21-534, SEP 1994, WILL BE USED.

PAGE 5

PART II - INFORMATION RELATING TO MARRIAGE (Continued)	
18. DATE OF BIRTH OF SURVIVING SPOUSE	19. WAS A CHILD BORN OF THE SURVIVING SPOUSE'S MARRIAGE TO THE VETERAN OR WAS A CHILD BORN TO THEM PRIOR TO THE SURVIVING SPOUSE'S MARRIAGE TO THE VETERAN? *(Complete only if the surviving spouse was married to the veteran for less than one year)*

20. DID SURVIVING SPOUSE LIVE CONTINUOUSLY WITH THE VETERAN FROM DATE OF MARRIAGE TO DATE OF DEATH?

☐ YE   ☐ NO *(If "NO," complete item 21)*

21. CAUSE OF SEPARATION *(Explain fully, giving reason, date of separation, duration, etc. If separation was by court order, attach a copy of such order)*

PART III - INFORMATION CONCERNING CHILDREN *(See Instructions, Paragraph J)*

IDENTIFICATION OF CHILDREN AND INFORMATION RELATIVE TO CUSTODY

NOTE - List below the name of each child of the veteran who is (1) under 18 years of age (or under 23 years of age if attending school) or (2) of any age if permanently incapable of self-support by reason of mental or physical defect. The term "child" includes an illegitimate, adopted, or stepchild of the veteran as well as any child whose marriage has been terminated by divorce, annulment, or death of a spouse. If the birth of a child of a veteran is expected, that fact should be stated.

22A. NAME OF CHILD *(First, middle initial, last)*	22B. DATE OF BIRTH *(Mo. day, yr.)*	22C. PLACE OF BIRTH *(CITY AND STATE)*	22D. SOCIAL SECURITY NO. OF CHILD	22E. IDENTIFY *(Check each applicable category)*				
				MARRIED PREVI-OUSLY	STEPCHILD OR ADOPTED	ILLEGI TIMATE	OVER 18 ATTENDING SCHOOL	SERIOUSLY DISABLED

23. NAME OF ANY CHILDREN NOT IN YOUR CUSTODY	24. MONTHLY AMOUNT YOU CONTRIBUTE TO CHILD'S SUPPORT
	$
	$
	$
	$

PART IV - NET WORTH OF SURVIVING SPOUSE AND/OR CHILD/REN *(See Instructions, Paragraph K)*

ITEM NO.	SOURCE	AMOUNTS				
		SURVIVING SPOUSE OR CUSTODIAN OF CHILDREN	NAME OF CHILD/REN			
25A.	STOCKS, BONDS, BANK DEPOSITS	$	$	$	$	$
25B.	REAL ESTATE *(Do not include residence)*	$	$	$	$	$
25C.	OTHER	$	$	$	$	$
25D.	NET WORTH	$	$	$	$	$

YOU MUST SIGN AND DATE THIS FORM AT THE BOTTOM OF PAGE 9.

PAGE 6

PART V INCOME OF SURVIVING SPOUSE AND/OR CHILDREN AND CUSTODIAN OF CHILD/REN
(Important - Carefully read paragraph L of Instructions before completing this section)

SOCIAL SECURITY

26A. HAVE YOU APPLIED FOR OR ARE YOU RECEIVING OR ENTITLED TO RECEIVE BENEFITS FROM THE SOCIAL SECURITY ADMINISTRATION ON YOUR OWN BEHALF OR ON BEHALF OF A CHILD/REN IN YOUR CUSTODY?	26B. BEGINNING DATE *(Month, year)*
☐ YE ☐ NO	

	MONTHLY	SURVIVING SPOUSE OR CUSTODIAN OF CHILDREN	EACH CHILD'S SHARE
26C.	AMOUNT OF MONTHLY SOCIAL SECURITY CHECK	$	$
26D.	ADDITIONAL MEDICARE DEDUCTIO		
26E.	TOTAL MONTHLY BENEFITS *(Sum of 26C and 26D)*	$	$

26F. IS SOCIAL SECURITY BASED ON YOUR OWN EMPLOYMENT?	26G. DO YOU EXPECT YOUR SOCIAL SECURITY BENEFITS TO INCREASE AS A RESULT OF THE VETERAN'S DEATH?
☐ YES ☐ NO	☐ YES ☐ NO

REPORT GROSS MONTHLY INCOME, BY SOURCE, INCLUDING ANY MONTHLY DEDUCTIONS FOR EACH FAMILY MEMBER

ITE NO.	SOURC	SURVIVIN SPOUSE OR DIAN OF	AMOUNT OF INCOME			BEGINNING DATE
			NAME OF			MONTH/YEAR
			NAME	NAME	NAME	
27A.	U.S. CIVIL		$	$	$	
27B.	U.S. RAILROAD		$	$	$	
27C	MILITARY		$	$	$	
27D.	BLACK LUNG		$	$	$	
27E.	SUPPLEMENTAL SECURITY INCOME/PUBLIC ASSISTANCE		$	$	$	
27F.	ALL OTHER INCOME (Specify source - for additional space, use Item 37, "Remarks")		$	$	$	

REPORT EXPECTED GROSS INCOME (OR ONE-TIME INCOME) FOR THE 12 MONTH PERIOD FROM DATE OF VETERAN'S DEATH OR, IF CLAIM IS FILED MORE THAN 45 DAYS AFTER THE VETERAN DIED, THE 12 MONTH PERIOD FROM THE DATE THE CLAIM IS SIGNED.

ITE NO.	SOURC	SURVIVIN SPOUSE OR DIAN OF	AMOUNT OF INCOME			BEGINNING DATE
			NAME OF CHILDREN			MONTH/YEAR
			NAME	NAME	NAME	
28A.	EARNING		$	$	$	
28B.	DIVIDENDS, INTEREST.		$	$	$	
28C.	LIFE		$	$	$	
28D.	ALL OTHER INCOME *(Specify source - for additional space, use Item 37, "Remarks")*		$	$	$	

YOU MUST SIGN AND DATE THIS FORM AT THE BOTTOM OF PAGE 9.

VA FORM JUN 1998 **21 -534**

OCT 1 993

PART VI - DEDUCTIBLE EXPENSES

NOTE: Your income may be reduced by the amount of unreimbursed expenses of the veteran's or his/her child's last illness and burial and the veteran's just debts which were paid by you. Be sure to report any reimbursement received on these expenses or debts. See paragraph N of instructions for reporting payments and reimbursements made after filing of your claim.

29A. NAME AND ADDRESS OF PERSON TO WHOM PAID	29B. TOTAL AMT. OF EXPENSE OR DEBT	29C. NATURE OF EXPENSE OR DEBT	29D. DATE PAID	29E. AMOUNT PAID BY YOU
	$			$
	$			$
	$			$
	$			$
	$			$
	$			$

PART VII - MISCELLANEOUS INFORMATION

30. HAS A SURVIVING SPOUSE OR CHILD FILED A CLAIM FOR COMPENSATION FROM THE OFFICE OF WORKER'S COMPENSATION PROGRAMS BECAUSE OF DEATH OF VETERAN ON WHOSE SERVICE THIS CLAIM IS FILED?

☐ YES ☐ NO

31. IS A CLAIM OR COURT ACTION PENDING OR HAS A COURT DECREE AWARDING DAMAGES ON A SETTLEMENT OR COMPROMISE OF A CLAIM BASED ON THE DEATH OF THE VETERAN BEEN MADE?

☐ YES ☐ NO *(If "YES," explain in Item 37, "Remarks")*

32. IS A CLAIM FOR SURVIVOR BENEFIT PLAN (SBP) ANNUITY FROM A SERVICE DEPARTMENT PENDING OR HAS AN AWARD OF THE SBP ANNUITY BEEN MADE BASED ON THE DEATH OF THE VETERAN?

☐ YES ☐ NO *(If "YES," explain in Item 37, "Remarks")*

33A. HAS THE SURVIVING SPOUSE OR CHILD FILED A CLAIM PREVIOUSLY WITH THE VA? ☐ YES ☐ NO *(If "YES, complete Items 33B through 35 inclusive)*	33B. NAME OF PERSON ON WHOSE SERVICE CLAIM WAS MADE	33C. RELATIONSHIP TO CLAIMANT
34. VA FILE NO.	35. OFFICE WHERE CLAIM WAS FILED *(City and state)*	

36A. ARE YOU NOW A PATIENT IN A NURSING HOME? ☐ YES ☐ NO *(If "YES", complete item 36B)*	36B. DOES MEDICAID COVER ALL OR PART OF YOUR NURSING HOME COSTS? ☐ YES ☐ NO *(If "YES," give the name and address of nursing home in Item 37, "Remarks")*

37. REMARKS *(If additional space is needed, attach separate sheet)*

PAGE 8

37. REMARKS *(Continued)*

PART VIII - DIRECT DEPOSIT INFORMATION

All Federal payments made to a person who applied and became eligible for benefit payments after July 26, 1996. must be made by electronic funds transfer (EFT). This requirement cannot be waived by the VA unless you certify that you do not have an account with a financial institution or an authorized payment agent. VA payments to you will be made EFT unless you certify that you do not have an account with a financial institution or an authorized payment agent. Please attach a voided personal check or deposit slip or provide all of the following information:

38. ACCOUNT NUMBER - PLEASE CHECK THE APPROPRIATE BOX AND PROVIDE THAT ACCOUNT NUMBER, IF APPLICABLE

☐ CHECKING   ☐ I CERTIFY THAT I DO NOT HAVE AN ACCOUNT WITH A FINANCIAL INSTITUTION OR CERTIFIED PAYMENT AGENT

☐ SAVINGS   ACCOUNT NUMBER

39. NAME OF FINANCIAL INSTITUTION

40. ROUTING OR TRANSIT NUMBER

CERTIFICATION AND AUTHORIZATION FOR RELEASE OF INFORMATION - I CERTIFY THAT the foregoing statements are true and complete to the best of my knowledge and belief. **I CONSENT THAT** any physician, surgeon, dentist, or hospital that has treated or examined me for any purpose, or that I have consulted professionally, may furnish to the **DEPARTMENT OF VETERANS AFFAIRS** any information about myself, and I waive any privilege which renders such information confidential.

41A. DAYTIME TELEPHONE NO. *(Include Area Code)*	41B. EVENING TELEPHONE NO. *(Include Area Code)*
42. SIGNATURE OF CLAIMANT. CUSTODIAN OR GUARDIAN	43. DATE SIGNED

WITNESS TO SIGNATURE OF CLAIMANT IF MADE BY "X" MARK

NOTE: Signature made by mark must be witnessed by two persons to whom the person making the statement is personally known. The signature and printed names and addresses of the witnesses must be shown.

44A. SIGNATURE AND PRINTED NAME OF WITNESS	44B. ADDRESS OF WITNESS
45A. SIGNATURE AND PRINTED NAME OF WITNESS	45B. ADDRESS OF WITNESS

PENALTY - The law provides severe penalties which include fine or imprisonment, or both, for the willful submission of any statement or evidence of a material fact, knowing it to be false. or for the fraudulent acceptance of any payment to which you are not entitled.

PAGE 9

OMB Approved No. 0960-0062

DEPARTMENT OF HEALTH AND HUMAN SERVICES	SOCIAL SECURITY ADMINISTRATION **APPLICATION FOR SURVIVORS BENEFITS** (PAYABLE UNDER TITLE II OF THE SOCIAL SECURITY ACT) IMPORTANT- Read instructions before completing form. Detach and retain ONLY the instruction sheet	(DO NOT WRITE IN THIS SPACE) VA DATE STAMP

1. FIRST NAME - MIDDLE NAME - LAST NAME OF VETERAN *(Type or print)*	2. DATE OF DEATH

NOTE: If the veteran's Social Security No. is unknown complete Items 4, 5, 6 and 7 about veteran.

3. SOCIAL SECURITY NO. OF VETERAN	4. DATE OF BIRTH	5. PLACE OF BIRTH

6. NAME OF FATHER	7. MAIDEN NAME OF MOTHER	8. DID THE VETERAN WORK IN THE RAILROAD INDUSTRY AT ANY TIME AFTER 1936? ☐ YES ☐ NO

NOTE: The following information should be furnished for each period of the veteran's active service (regular or reserves) after September 7, 1939, in the military service of the United States or service as a commissioned officer in the Public Health Service or the National Oceanic and Atmospheric Administration or during WWII, Philippine or Filipino or Allied country military service. If additional space is needed, attach a separate sheet.

9A. DATE ENTERED ACTIVE SERVICE	9B. SERVICE NO.	9C. DATE SEPARATED FROM ACTIVE SERVICE	9D. GRADE, RANK, OR RATING, ORGANIZATION AND BRANCH OF SERVICE

10. RELATIONSHIP OF APPLICANT TO VETERAN ☐ SURVIVING SPOUSE ☐ CHILD ☐ PARENT	11. DATE OF BIRTH OF APPLICANT	12. VA FILE NO.

CHILDREN: Show name of surviving children (including natural children, adopted children and stepchildren) or dependent grandchildren (Including stepgrandchildren) who at any time since the veteran died, were unmarried and (a) under age 18; (b) age 18 to 19 and attending secondary school; (c) disabled or handicapped (18 or over and disability been before age 22).

13A.	13B.
13C.	13D.

I know that anyone who makes or causes to be made a false statement or representation of a material fact in an application or for use in determining a right to payment under the Social Security Act commits a crime punishable under Federal law by fine, imprisonment, or both. I affirm that all information I have given in this document is true.

14. DATE *(Month,day,year)*	15. SIGNATURE OF APPLICANT *(First name, middle Initial, last name) (Sign in ink)* SIGN ▶ HERE

16. MAILING ADDRESS OF APPLICANT *(No. and street or rural route, city or P.O., State and ZIP Code)*	17. TELEPHONE NO. *(Include Area Code)*

WITNESSES REQUIRED ONLY IF SIGNATURE OF APPLICANT IS MADE BY "X" MARK ABOVE

18A. SIGNATURE OF WITNESS	18B. ADDRESS OF WITNESS *(No.and street, city, State and ZIP Code)*
19A. SIGNATURE OF WITNESS	19B. ADDRESS OF WITNESS *(No.and street, city, State and ZIP Code)*

ITEMS BELOW TO BE COMPLETED BY THE DEPARTMENT OF VETERANS AFFAIRS Use reverse for "Remarks"

20. PROOFS RECEIVED	21. PROOFS REQUESTED FROM CLAIMANT OR OTHER *(Specify)*
☐ DEATH ☐ MARRIAGE	☐ DEATH ☐ MARRIAGE
☐ AGE _____ (NAME)	☐ AGE _____ (NAME)
☐ OTHER *(Specify)* _____ (NAME)	☐ OTHER *(Specify)* _____ (NAME)
_____ (NAME)	_____ (NAME)

22. DATE	23. NAME AND ADDRESS OF TRANSMITTING VA OFFICE

SSA-24, NOV 1992

PAGE 11

IMPORTANT: PLEASE READ THE FOLLOWING BEFORE YOU COMPLETE THE SSA-24.
INSTRUCTIONS FOR COMPLETING FORM SSA-24, APPLICATION FOR SURVIVORS

BENEFITS (Payable Under Title II of the Social Security Act)

This application form, SSA-24, is an Application for Survivors Benefits Payable under Title II of the Social Security Act, as amended. Under authority of section 202(o) of the Social Security Act the application requests information in order to determine eligibility to social security benefits.

You do not have to complete this application; there are no penalties under the law if you do not complete part or all of the SSA-24. However, it is usually to your advantage to provide the information because not providing it could prevent an accurate and timely decision on your claim or could result in the loss of some benefits or insurance coverage.

If you do wish to supply the information requested on the SSA-24, this information will be forwarded to the Social Security Administration and used by them to determine whether social security benefits may be payable to surviving dependent(s) of the veteran. Social Security will then contact you regarding any social security benefits payable based on information given on this form.

Please understand that Social Security may, in certain instances, disclose the information on this form to another Federal, State or local agency or individual without your written consent. This would be done in order to:

enable a third party or an agency to assist Social Security in establishing an individual's right to benefits or coverage;

comply with Federal laws which require or authorize the release of information from social security records; and

facilitate statistical research and audit activities necessary to assure the integrity and improvement of the social security programs.

If you should have any question about entitlement to social security benefits or the information you have provided on this form, please contact your local social security office.

Complete each item of the attached application, Form SSA-24, (except the Items 20 through 23). When signed and dated the form SHOULD BE LEFT ATTACHED to your completed VA Form 21-534, Application for Dependency and Indemnity Compensation, Death Pension and Accrued Benefits by a Surviving Spouse or Child (Including Death Compensation if Applicable).

PAGE 12

GLOSSARY

Accounting—The record of transactions in connection with the administration of a decedent's estate filed by the executor with the court.

Acknowledgement—A formal declaration of one's signature before a notary public.

Actuary—One who computes various insurance and property costs, and calculates the cost of life insurance risks and insurance premiums.

Administrator—The person appointed by the court to settle the estate of a deceased person if he or she dies intestate.

Affidavit—A sworn or affirmed statement made in writing and signed; if sworn, it is notarized.

American Bar Association (ABA)—A national organization of lawyers and law students.

American Civil Liberties Union (ACLU)—A nationwide organization dedicated to the enforcement and preservation of rights and civil liberties guaranteed by the federal and state constitutions.

Asset—The entirety of a person's property, either real or personal.

Assignee—An assignee is a person to whom an assignment is made, also known as a grantee.

Assignment—An assignment is the transfer of an interest in a right or property from one party to another.

Attestation—The act of witnessing an instrument in writing at the request of the party making the same, and subscribing it as a witness.

Attorney In Fact—An attorney-in-fact is an agent or representative of another given authority to act in that person's name and place pursuant to a document called a "power of attorney."

Beneficiary—A person who is designated to receive property upon the death of another, such as the beneficiary of a life insurance policy, who receives the proceeds upon the death of the insured.

Bequest—Refers to a gift of personal property contained in a will.

Bill of Rights—The first eight amendments to the United States Constitution.

Bond—A certificate issued by a company or governmental body which represents a debt owed to the bondholder, who receives interest while the debt is outstanding at a specified rate. On the maturity date of the bond, the bondholder is repaid the debt.

Capacity—Capacity is the legal qualification concerning the ability of one to understand the nature and effects of one's acts.

Chattel—Article of personal property.

Codicil—A document modifying an existing will which, in order to be valid, must be formally drafted and witnessed according to statutory requirements.

Community Property—A form of ownership in a minority of states where a husband and wife are deemed to own property in common, including earnings, each owning an undivided one-half interest in the property.

Consanguinity—Related by blood.

Coroner—The public official whose responsibility it is to investigate the circumstances and causes of deaths which occur within his or her jurisdiction.

Decedent—A deceased person.

Decree—A decision or order of the court.

Disclaim—To refuse to accept a gift or bequest.

Deductible—An amount an insured person must pay before they are entitled to recover money from the insurer, in connection with a loss or expense covered by an insurance policy.

Deed—A legal instrument conveying title to real property.

Dividends—A payment which a corporation makes to its shareholders according to the number of shares outstanding.

Domicile—The one place designated as an individual's permanent home.

Due Process Rights—All rights which are of such fundamental importance as to require compliance with due process standards of fairness and justice.

Durable Power of Attorney—Also known as a "health care proxy," refers to a document naming a person to make a medical decisions in the event that the individual becomes unable to make those decisions himself or herself.

Duress—Refers to the action of one person which compels another to do something he or she would not otherwise do.

Duty—The obligation, to which the law will give recognition and effect, to conform to a particular standard of conduct toward another.

Earned Income—Income which is gained through one's labor and services, as opposed to investment income.

Elective Share—Statutory provision that a surviving spouse may choose between taking that which is provided in the spouse's will, or taking a statutorily prescribed share.

Employee Retirement Income Security Act of 1974 (ERISA)—A federal statute which governs the administration of pension plans.

Equitable Distribution—The power of the courts to equitably distribute all property legally and beneficially acquired during marriage by either spouse, whether legal title lies in their joint or individual names.

Escheat—The reversion of private property to the government under certain conditions, e.g. the absence of an heir.

Escrow—The arrangement for holding instruments or money which is not to be released until certain specified conditions are met.

Estate—The entirety of one's property, real or personal.

Estate Tax—A tax levied on a decedent's estate in connection with the right to transfer property after death.

Execution—The performance of all acts necessary to render a written instrument complete, such as signing, sealing, acknowledging, and delivering the instrument; also refers to supplementary proceedings to enforce a judgment, which, if monetary, involves a direction to the sheriff to take the necessary steps to collect the judgment.

Executor—A person appointed by the maker of a will to carry out his or her wishes concerning the administration and distribution of his or estate according to the terms of a will.

Executor's Deed—A deed given by an executor or other fiduciary which conveys real property.

Exemption—A tax deduction granted a taxpayer who has a certain status, e.g. aged 65 or over.

Face Value—The value of an insurance policy upon the death of the insured.

Fee Simple Absolute—A real property estate giving the owner the most absolute power over the title available.

Fiduciary—A fiduciary is a person having a legal duty, created by an undertaking, to act primarily for the benefit of another in matters connected with the undertaking.

Fixed Income—Income which is unchangeable.

Fraudulent Conveyance—The transfer of property for the purpose of delaying or defrauding creditors.

Gift Tax—A tax assessed against the transferor of a gift of property, based upon the fair market value of the property on the date transferred.

Grace Period—In contract law, a period specified in a contract which is beyond the due date but during which time payment will be accepted without penalty.

Grantee—One who receives a conveyance of real property by deed.

Grantor—One who conveys real property by deed.

Guardian—A person who is entrusted with the management of the property and/or person of another who is incapable, due to age or incapacity, to administer their own affairs.

Guardian Ad Litem—Person appointed by a court to represent a minor or incompetent for purpose of some litigation

Heir—One who inherits property.

Heirs—Those individuals who, by law, inherit an estate of an ancestor who dies without a will.

Hereditament—Anything which can be inherited.

Hereditary Succession—The passing of title to an estate according to the laws of descent.

Illegal—Against the law.

Incapacity—Incapacity is a defense to breach of contract which refers to a lack of legal, physical or intellectual power to enter into a contract.

Incompetency—Lack of legal qualification or fitness to discharge a legally required duty or to handle one's own affairs; also refers to matters not admissible in evidence.

Indigent—A person who is financially destitute.

Inherit—To take as an heir at law by descent rather than by will.

Inheritance—Property inherited by heirs according to the laws of descent and distribution.

Inheritance Tax—A tax levied on heirs in connection with the right to receive property from a decedent's estate.

Insurance—A contingency agreement, supported by consideration, whereby the insured receives a benefit, e.g. money, in the event the contingency occurs.

Inter Vivos—Latin for "between the living." Refers to transactions made during the lifetime of the parties.

Intestate—The state of dying without having executed a valid will.

Intestate Succession—The manner of disposing of property according to the laws of descent and distribution when the decedent died without leaving a valid will.

Irrevocable Trust—A trust that cannot be canceled by the person who established it.

Joint Tenancy—The ownership of property by two or more persons who each have an undivided interest in the whole property, with the right of survivorship, whereby upon the death of one joint tenant, the remaining joint tenants assume ownership.

Legacy—A gift of personal property by will.

Legal Capacity—Referring to the legal capacity to sue, it is the requirement that a person bringing the lawsuit have a sound mind, be of lawful age, and be under no restraint or legal disability.

Legatee—One who takes a legacy.

Letters of Administration—A formal document issued by a court which authorizes a person to act as an administrator for the estate of a deceased person.

Life Estate—An estate in land held during the term of a specified person's life.

Life Insurance—A contract between an insured and an insurer whereby the insurer promises to pay a sum of money upon the death of the insured to his or her designated beneficiary, in return for the periodic payment of money, known as a premium.

Living Trust—A trust which is operated during the life of the creator of the trust.

Living Will—A declaration that states an individual's wishes concerning the use of extraordinary life support systems.

Marital Property—Property purchased by persons while married to each other.

Maturity Date—The date upon which a creditor is designated to receive payment of a debt, such as payment of the principal value of a bond to a bondholder by the issuing company or governmental entity.

Minor—A person who has not yet reached the age of legal competence, which is designated as 18 in most states.

Net Estate—The gross estate less the decedent's debts, funeral expenses and any other deductions proscribed by law.

Net Income—Gross income less deductions and exemptions proscribed by law.

Net Worth—The difference between one's assets and liabilities.

Nonfreehold Estate—A leasehold.

Note—A writing which promises payment of a debt.

Notice of Petition—Written notice of a petitioner that a hearing will be held in a court to determine the relief requested in an annexed petition.

Oath—A sworn declaration of the truth under penalty of perjury.

Party—Person having a direct interest in a legal matter, transaction or proceeding.

Pecuniary Gift—A bequest in a will of a stated amount of money.

Pension Benefits—An amount of money paid to an employee upon retirement based upon such factors as salary and length of employment.

Personal Representative—The executor or administrator of a decedent's estate.

Petition—A formal written request to a court which initiates a special proceeding.

Petitioner—In a special proceeding, one who commences a formal written application, requesting some action or relief, addressed to a court for determination.

Portfolio—The entirety of one's financial investments.

Power of Attorney—A legal document authorizing another to act on one's behalf.

Probate—The process of proving the validity of a will and administering the estate of a decedent.

Real Estate—The land and all the things permanently attached to it.

Real Property—Land, and generally whatever is erected or growing upon or affixed to the land.

Residuary Clause—The clause in a will which conveys to the residuary beneficiaries any property of the testator which was not specifically given to a particular legatee.

Shareholder—A person who owns shares of stock in a corporation.

Specific Gift—A gift bequest in a will of a specific piece of property.

Statute—A law.

Stock Certificate—A certificate issued to a shareholder which evidences partial ownership of the shareholder in a company.

Succession—The process by which a decedent's property is distributed, either by will or by the laws of descent and distribution.

Successor—One who takes the place of another and continues in their position.

Surety—A surety is one who undertakes to pay money or perform in the event that the principal fails to do so.

Surrogate—A person appointed to act in place of another.

Survival Statute—A statute that preserves for a decedent's estate a cause of action for infliction of pain and suffering and related damages suffered up to the moment of death.

Taxable Estate—The decedent's gross estate less applicable statutory estate tax deductions, such as charitable deductions.

Tenancy by the Entirety—A form of ownership available only to a husband and wife whereby they each are deemed to hold title to the whole property, with right of survivorship.

Tenancy in Common—An ownership of real estate by two or more persons, each of whom has an undivided fractional interest in the whole property, without any right of survivorship.

Testament—Another name for a will.

Testamentary—Of or by a will.

Testate—The state of dying with a valid will in place.

Testator—A male individual who makes and executes a will.

Testatrix—A female individual who makes and executes a will.

Testify—The offering of a statement in a judicial proceeding, under oath and subject to the penalty of perjury.

Testimony—The sworn statement make by a witness in a judicial proceeding.

Title—In property law, denotes ownership and the right to possess real property.

Trust—The transfer of property, real or personal, to the care of a trustee, with the intention that the trustee manage the property on behalf of another person.

Uniform Laws—Laws that have been approved by the Commissioners on Uniform State Laws, and which are proposed to all state legislatures for consideration and adoption.

Uniform Transfers to Minors Act—Law that allows gifts to minors through a custodian.

Waiver—An intentional and voluntary surrender of a right.

Ward—A person over whom a guardian is appointed to manage his or her affairs.

Will—A legal document which a person executes setting forth their wishes as to the distribution of their property upon death.

Witness—One who testifies to what he has seen, heard, or otherwise observed.

X—Refers to the mark that may be used to denote one's signature when the signer is unable to write his or her name.

BIBLIOGRAPHY AND ADDITIONAL RESOURCES

American Association of Retired Persons (AARP) (Date Visited: June 2003) <http://www.aarp.org/>.

ABA Real Property, Probate and Trust Law Section (Date Visited: June 2003) <http://www.abanet.or/>.

Black's Law Dictionary, Fifth Edition. St. Paul, MN: West Publishing Company, 1979.

Internal Revenue Service (Date Visited: June 2003) <http://www.irs.ustreas.gov/>.

Cornell Legal Information Institute (Date Visited: June 2003) <http://www.law.cornell.edu/>.

National Academy of Elder Law Attorneys (Date Visited: June 2003) <http://www.naela.org/>.

National Center for Health Statistics (Date Visited: June 2003) <http://www.cdc.gov/nchswww/howto/w2w/w2welcom.htm/>.

National Senior Citizens Law Center (Date Visited: June 2003) <http://www.nsclc.org/>.

Social Security Administration (Date Visited: June 2003) <http://www.socialsecurity.gov/>.

Uniform Probate Code Locator (Date Visited: June 2003) <http://www.law.cornell.edu/uniform/probate.html/>.

United States Veterans Administration (Date Visited: June 2003) <http://www.va.gov/>.